HISTORIC
COUNTRY INNS
OF CALIFORNIA

HISTORIC
COUNTRY INNS
OF CALIFORNIA

Jim Crain

CHRONICLE BOOKS   SAN FRANCISCO

Library of Congress Cataloging in Publication Data

Crain, Jim.
  Historic country inns of California.
  1. Hotels, taverns, etc.—California—Directories
I. Title.
TX907.C73   647'.95794   77-727
ISBN 0-87701-088-9
ISBN 0-87701-208-3

Cover photo by Curt Bruce.
Composition by Hansen & Associates.
Book design by Jane Vandenburgh.
Cartography by Milne.

Chronicle Books
870 Market Street
San Francisco, Ca. 94102

All photographs by the author, or from the author's
collection, except for the following: Historical Collection, Title Insurance and Trust Company, pages 10,
163, 164; Bancroft Library, page 128; John Oldenkamp, page 169. Special thanks to the California Historical Society for the use of the Ralph H. Cross
Collection.

Historic Country Inns

TABLE OF CONTENTS

Tourists traveled by stagecoach over dusty, pitted roads to reach the Mammoth Grove Hotel at Calaveras Big Trees.

INTRODUCTION

I became fascinated with California's historic country inns several years ago, returning from an off-season camping trip in the mountains. The day turned into a windy, rainy dusk as I drove cautiously from curve to curve along the twisting, tortuous route back to civilization. Rain pounded on the windshield, and my pace was getting me nowhere. After a long day's hike on the trail, I didn't feel like pushing on.

In the next small town I spotted what seemed to be the only lodging around, a rather charming Victorian hotel, and the sign said "Vacancy." Fantastic! But then it was hardly the summer tourist season. A friendly woman greeted me when I entered the ancient lobby. My curiosity got the best of me as I surveyed the memorabilia-covered walls, and my hostess seemed eager and proud to relate the inn's captivating history. After signing the old-fashioned register and partaking of the evening's home-cooked meal, I climbed the creaky red-carpeted stairs to my room on the second floor. The smells of antiquity were everywhere, and the furnishings were from another era. I sank down on the big brass bed to reflect on this relic from the past century that I had stumbled upon. Steam pipes rattled, limbs scraped against the window panes and rain beat on the tin roof with a most soothing steadiness—these were sounds I hadn't heard since my boyhood days on a farm in Texas.

I like the old inns because they reflect a particularly colorful era. It's an era I never knew, but one that I can feel each time I indulge in a weekend escape to bygone places. These relics are all that remain of the thousands of rustic inns, lodges and

Primitive accommodations such as those at Hutchings House did not deter adventurers from making arduous trips into the magnificent Yosemite Valley.

hotels that once dotted the California countryside. The best and most intriguing are gone, and I regret their passing for they were exciting places. Digging up the histories of these places has given me a new insight into the way of life at the early hostelries and the people who sought their hospitality and charm.

When the great Gold Rush faded, the rugged miners in the north country were replaced by an inquisitive band of tourists that scoured every inch of the lusty frontier for sights as good as gold. They traveled as far as they could by rail, and then continued their rambles into the countryside aboard rickety stagecoaches, stopping for the night at way-

The Glendale Villa Hotel at Glendale was one of the big fancy hotels that sprang up in small towns. They were usually the most ornate buildings for miles around and were rather spectacular in their barren settings.

side inns. They were headed for the grand mountain lodges and coastal resorts, the relaxing mineral spring spas and a multitude of country hotels that would satisfy their adventurous moods for days and weeks at a time.

Vacationing at one of these tranquil retreats meant loafing and participating in peaceful outdoor experiences that were unobtainable back in the city. Proper ladies sunned themselves in bustled, over-abundant bathing costumes on the sandy beaches and teamed up for the genteel sports of archery, croquet, and rowing. Men followed more adventurous pursuits, exploring the depths of mysterious

caves or scouting the wilderness for promising fishing holes. Together, they enjoyed "shooting the chutes" and gazing at a variety of scenic wonders that only the California landscape could provide. In the evening the inn fed them, entertained them and generally served as a center for country gregariousness.

Travelers met fellow travelers and traded tales of the great sights they had seen. Fact and fiction were freely bantered about, and some of the colorful stories involved the hostelries themselves. It's said, for instance, that the hotel in the northern Sierra town of Woodleaf had the first indoor toilet in the area. Overcurious people beat a path to the second floor just to watch someone pull the chain. They shook their heads in amazement and disdain as the water rushed in and out, and they vowed never to own one of the ridiculous contraptions.

Nineteen hundred rolled around and the thrill of "autoing" came into vogue. The fledgling machines weren't much more comfortable than the bumpy overland stages they replaced but they did offer a sense of freedom from schedules and a way to reach some previously inaccessible backcountry. This new mobility created a need for more and more inns as more and more travelers hit the road. Every little town had its friendly hotel, needed because people spent so much time getting from place to place. It took three or four days to travel from San Diego to San Francisco along the inland route, even at a smart thirty-five miles per hour on the straightaways.

In the rural villages, the hotel was usually the largest and most stately building in town and a sign of community prosperity. It was a vital part of the cultural scene, since its clientele often ranged from presidents to outlaws. From the hotels, guests would send penny postcards to the folks back home with such messages as, "We missed seeing Teddy Roosevelt by three days, but slept in his bed."

These turn-of-the-century hostelries had character and charm, and they all looked quite handsome in their pastoral settings. Some were simple basic buildings of the Monterey style, and good examples of the state's frontier architecture. Others were fancifully ornate structures highly representative of the Victorian style. They joined their earlier counterparts —the famous Gold Rush hotels, the adobe-style lodges and the quaint coastal inns that had served wayfarers for so long—in expressing the various changing trends in California architecture.

These were grand old buildings, the creations of a time when nature had an unspoiled meaning to it —fresh air, blue skies and a lot of uncrowded countryside. This era actually was the "good old days," so I'm told. I've found that the good old days are not as lost as we may think. In my efforts to uncover the historic stagecoach inns that are still in use, I've stumbled onto some real finds. They're all capable of stimulating our nostalgic sensibilities and providing us a chance to relive, at least briefly, the romance of an earlier era. Some of these buildings have always catered to travelers; others have been transformed to perform that function. But hospitable innkeepers have perpetuated the history and taken care to preserve the atmosphere of bygone days so that the overnight hours can become an extension of the adventure of exploring California's past. And what a past it was.

A few words on how to use the information in this book might be helpful. Most of the inns mentioned here are very popular during the summer, so reservations may be required weeks or even months in advance. For certain holidays reservations a year in advance may be necessary. However, during the

The Hotel Del Monte on the Monterey Peninsula was one of several prestigious resort spas that dotted the California coastline.

winter some rooms remain unoccupied even on weekends, depending on the particular inn and its location. Weekday chances are usually good no matter what the season.

Rates change so rapidly that only a general price range for each establishment is given here. The rates are usually based on double occupancy, European plan accommodations (meals not included). Classifications are *inexpensive*, $10 to $28; *moderate*, $28 to $50; and *expensive*, $50 and up. Some inns operate on the American plan (meals included), which can increase the rate. European or American plan is designated for each entry.

Most inns welcome children but discourage pets. Inquire when making a reservation.

The
North Coast

TO OREGON

Eureka

SCOTIA
INN
Scotia

DINSMORE
LODGE

TO RED BLUFF

BENBOW
INN   Garberville

DEHAVEN VALLEY
FARM

Westport

GREY WHALE INN
BLUE ROSE INN
CASA DEL NOYO

Fort Bragg

Willits

JOSHUA GRINDLE INN
MacCALLUM HOUSE
MENDOCINO HOTEL
MENDOCINO VILLAGE
INN

Mendocino
GLENDEVEN
LITTLE RIVER
INN

TO SACRAMENTO

HERITAGE
HOUSE

Elk
ELK
COVE
INN

Ukiah

HARBOR
HOUSE

OLD MILANO
HOTEL

Gualala

Cloverdale

Jenner

TO SAN FRANCISCO

THE NORTH COAST

I've stood on the edge of the continent many times, captivated by the Pacific surf pounding onto the rugged shoreline below. This vast stretch of north coast scenery is the longest strip of unspoiled coastline in the nation. It is interrupted only by a few sleepy fishing villages and old lumber towns that have dwindled to mere shadows of the thriving communities they once were.

Between the Oregon border and Eureka, giant redwoods—the tallest trees on earth—add their beauty to the dramatic coastline. South of Eureka, Highway 101 swings inland through the redwoods of southern Humboldt County. The best route for seeing the impressive groves is along the Avenue of the Giants, between Scotia and Garberville. This section of the old highway meanders more or less parallel with the freeway. The pace on the route is much slower than on the freeway and is more conducive to a full appreciation of the majestic trees. Pleasant back roads west of the freeway lead to Shelter Cove and through the Mattole Valley where some of the most isolated and least visited sections of coastline are to be found.

At Leggett, Highway 1 branches from Highway 101, and the route drops to the sea again. The Coast Highway hugs the hillsides as it winds along the brink of the oceanside cliffs from Rockport to the mouth of the Russian River. Scattered along the coast are plenty of interesting diversions. Fort Bragg is noted for its lumber mill tour and for the "Skunk" Railroad that rambles eastward through forty miles of countryside toward the inland town of Willits. At Russian Gulch and Van Damme state parks, the oddity of giant redwoods and cypress pygmy forest growing in close proximity to each other is a strange and memorable sight. Fort Ross, twelve miles north of Jenner, is the reconstruction of an early Russian settlement.

The spot most often visited along the north coast is the quaint little village of Mendocino, a seaside town built entirely of wood. No concrete or stucco buildings intrude to mar its charm. The Victorian, New England-style architecture of the weathered old buildings dates back to the 1880s. Mendocino is a haven for artists and craftsmen, and some tourists come particularly to enjoy its shops, galleries and restaurants. Its appeal to the tourists is so great that many residents fear the town's delicate character will succumb to the commercialism that has plagued similarly enticing communities. The inns around Mendocino are very popular during the summer and advance planning is advisable.

Weather along the north coast is somewhat unpredictable. Beautiful summer days can become overcast very suddenly when the offshore fogbank decides to pounce. Rain falls from November to May, and raging winter storms can grow fierce, but interesting. The inns that remain open during this time are relatively uncrowded. Visitors have the best chances for finding ideal weather conditions during late spring and early autumn.

DINSMORE LODGE

DINSMORE

On a recent journey to the north coast, my fondness for back roads carried me east along the weaving ribbon of asphalt called Highway 36, which leads into the Trinity foothills. Much of this impressive all-year route between U.S. 101 and Dinsmore parallels the Van Duzen River—quite a peaceful waterway in summer, but wild in winter. The journey along Highway 36 is an encounter with the dense towering redwoods, narrow one-lane bridges and weathered wooden barns that so admirably complement the countryside.

Forty-four miles from the junction with Highway 101 is the Dinsmore Lodge, located in the small Humboldt County community of Dinsmore. The town itself is not much more than a wide place in the road. The lodge is operated by Corky Korkowski and Bill Hulse, who commute between their successful Los Angeles design firm and the lodge, and by Art Eddy, their resident manager. Korkowski and Hulse stumbled onto the ramshackle, long-neglected resort a few years ago and, in spite of its dilapidated condition, were hooked by the challenge of its potential. In the course of completely restoring the old buildings, they shied away from creating what could have been a highly commercial and exploitive venture in favor of maintaining the historic atmosphere of the lodge and the quality of life it offers. The results should be inspiring to preservationists.

Certain county records suggest that the lodge was built around 1901 on the site of a Wintun Indian village, but recollections of recent guests indicate it may have been built even earlier, perhaps in the late 1890s. Until the Benbow Inn was built in the mid-twenties, Dinsmore Lodge was the largest resort in Humboldt County and a popular stagecoach stop between Eureka and Red Bluff. Travel through the area got a boost in 1913, when the "Three States Good Roads Rally" was held at the Lodge to celebrate the completion of Highway 36. Governors and their representatives from California, Oregon and Washington gathered for a venison lunch under the trees. Afterwards, the row of twenty-two automobiles made an impressive display as the dignitaries posed for photographs.

Old-timer John Friend, of nearby Hydesville, still recalls how, in 1917, he drove a horse-drawn stage over the Eureka-Red Bluff route and stopped each trip for a welcome lunch and fresh team at Dinsmore's. Later, in the twenties, motor-stages traveling eastward from Eureka and westward from Red Bluff would meet at the lodge. After lunch, the drivers would exchange passengers and continue to their destinations.

The central building is the main lodge, with its bright new coat of yellow paint and white trim. The big living room has a warm friendly fireplace, and upstairs are eight guest rooms. Korkowski compares the setting with a trip to grandmother's house—turn-of-the-century furnishings, bathroom down the hall, old-fashioned hospitality.

Out back are several guest cabins, built around 1934, and one particularly charming cottage with a moss-covered roof. Some of the cabins near the lodge have been restored and given new interiors; others along the river are currently receiving the same treatment.

The lodge is a lazy, peaceful place to pass some idle days of leisure. The way of life here is centered around all sorts of self-generated activities that are unattainable back in the city. The river is a magnetic source of pleasure for swimming or just floating on innertubes, and the riverbanks are perfect for nighttime cookouts. The surrounding mountain landscape is the backdrop for everything from day-dreaming in a meadow to cross-country skiing.

No meals are served in the lodge, but a small restaurant nearby provides adequate fare. The cabins are equipped with kitchens, and guests should bring their own utensils.

The owners are having fun piecing together the history of the old resort. It seems to unfold more and more as people who were guests in the early days hear of its reopening and return for a nostalgic visit.

Dinsmore Lodge, Dinsmore 95526. (707) 574-6466. Twenty miles south of Eureka on U.S. 101, then 44 miles east on Highway 36. Open all year. Lodging only; inexpensive to moderate. Eight lodge rooms with community bath; several housekeeping cabins. Restaurant and market across the highway. Airstrip, games, river sports, cross-country skiing, mountains and forests easily accessible. Lodge sits beside the Van Duzen River. Swimming, fishing, boating and nature trails at Ruth Reservoir 16 miles east.

SCOTIA INN

SCOTIA

Scotia claims the distinction of being one of the few remaining company-owned towns in America. The company is Pacific Lumber, established in 1869 and the largest redwood mill in the world. Tours of the mill have long been the town's number one attraction. Watching the hydraulic hoses debark the logs and the screaming saws rip them into slabs is an awesome experience.

The famed Scotia Inn once housed millworkers in the robust days of the lumberjacks. The original Scotia Hotel of 1889 sat beside the busy stage route between San Francisco and points north. It was torn down and rebuilt in 1924, reopening as the Mowatoc Inn. "Mowatoc" is an Indian name for the country where the Modoc and other Indian tribes lived. The millworkers were housed and fed at the inn, but by 1949 most of the single men had married and moved to more accommodating quarters, so the inn was given a new look to appeal to vacationers venturing into the redwood country. By then it had become known as the Scotia Inn.

I used to stay at the inn during my explorations along the Avenue of the Giants, the slower-paced parkway that parallels the freeway and winds through overwhelming groves of towering redwoods. But the rooms are no longer open to the public. It seems that Highway 101 has speeded up the pace and cut the travel time from San Francisco in half, so travelers continue on to more distant points. However, the Scotian Room is still a fine dining room, serving meals to travelers in the spirit of lumberjack days. The decor is Scottish, with an emphasis on big wooden beams and columns. The menu has almost two dozen entrees to choose from, including Humboldt Salmon, Bombay fillet tips, broiled lamb chops, shrimp creole and prime rib, all served with a relish plate, soup, salad and dessert.

On your way out through the impressive, two-story lobby notice the maple tree growing out of the redwood stump in front of the inn. A bird dropped a maple seed into the stump around 1900, and the seed took root. The oddity has since been featured in Ripley's "Believe It Or Not."

Scotia Inn, Scotia 95565. (707) 764-5683. Twenty-six miles south of Eureka on U.S. 101. Restaurant only. Dinner Wednesday through Friday, 5:30 P.M.–9 P.M.; Saturday, 5:30 P.M.–10 P.M; Sunday, 5 P.M.–9 P.M. Closed Monday and Tuesday.

BENBOW INN

GARBERVILLE

Folks thought the Benbows were out of their minds when the family decided to build an elegant hotel, complete with golf course and dam, in this seldom-traveled, lumber-producing area of California. But the rural peaceful valley in southern Humboldt County was enough to attract the four brothers and five sisters back to the land they had once called home. Here they bought two thousand acres along the banks of the south fork of the Eel River near Garberville. This was in 1924, and in spite of public opinion the Benbows channelled all their energy and imagination into the construction of one of California's finest resorts.

To insure success, they enlisted the services of Albert Farr, a San Francisco architect well known in the Bay Area for his shingle-style and half-timbered houses, the most notable being Jack London's Wolf House near Glen Ellen. The beautiful Tudor English inn that Farr conceived for the Benbows made quite a contrast with the forested countryside. It had a white stucco exterior sitting on a stone base and was embellished inside and out with fancy hand-carved woodwork. Such frills would cost a fortune today.

By 1926 the craftsmen were putting the finishing touches on the structure and its landscaping, and a challenging golf course was completed just in time for the first guests to tee off. The inn soon became a popular playground. Vacationers spent days and weeks at a time enjoying activities provided by the Benbows. Unlike today's nomadic travelers keeping pace with the speed of their automobiles, people were more inclined to vacation in one spot in those days. Famous people were often among the crowds —such celebrities as Eleanor Roosevelt, Herbert Hoover, John Barrymore, Charles Laughton, and Clara Bow.

After a long period of success, hard times forced the inn to close in the 1950s. The resort could have faded into oblivion except for the concern of Mr. and Mrs. Arthur Stadler, previous owners who gradually restored its former elegance and re-established its popularity. Chuck and Patsy Watts are the new owners of the Benbow, carrying on the same tradition of hospitality.

I discovered the inn on an autumn trip to explore the Mattole River back roads. On that first visit I arrived just in time for dinner. The large dining room with its wood-beamed ceiling and hardwood floors is an enjoyable place for any meal. A row of French doors open onto a delightful dining terrace shaded by overhanging trees and umbrellas. I splurged and had the menu's finest, Lobster Mornay cooked in sherry and a Cheddar cheese sauce. And it was superb.

It rained an unexpected rain the night I arrived, and the sudden downpour sent guests scurrying from the outdoor patio. The next morning was clear and sunny, and leftover patches of fog drifted through the tree tops. There doesn't seem to be an off-season here, since each change in the weather has its own appeal.

After breakfast, I set out to explore every nook and cranny of the inn and its patios, then went for a walk along the placid river, which comes to life with the winter rains. The inn itself is more alive than ever now, and it's good to see the old place enjoying the popularity it knew in its earlier years.

Benbow Inn, Garberville 95440. (707) 923-2124. Two miles south of Garberville on U.S. 101. Lodging on the European plan; inexpensive to moderate. All rooms with private baths. Closed January 1 to April 1. Dining room open to the public. All meals and Sunday brunch served. Nine-hole golf course, swimming, biking, giant redwoods nearby. Boating and fishing at Benbow Lake State Recreation Area.

DEHAVEN VALLEY FARM

WESTPORT

I especially like country farms, since I spent the first eighteen years of my life on one. I like the serene, pastoral settings, the sounds and smells of domestic animals, and the buildings—the barns, silos and farmhouses. But our house had nothing like the Victorian beauty of Dehaven Valley Farm, just north of Westport. The house was once the headquarters for a productive 7000-acre ranch, and it is very typical of the quaint farmhouses that dot the coastline north of Fort Bragg. The building shows up in old photos taken in 1890, so it's been around at least since then.

The farm's elegance was handsomely restored by the previous owners, Jim and Rachel Sears. Before they started work on it the house had been vacant for several years while the birds and bats enjoyed free reign. The Searses' motivation was the desire to create the kind of inn they had long searched for themselves, a place of great peace and seclusion away from tourist crowds and busy main streets. Ron Albrecht and Harry Cowan are the new owners. Guests who enjoyed the hospitality and atmosphere created by the Searses will find the experience is still the same.

The six upstairs guest rooms, with their slanted ceilings, are furnished with nice old country farmhouse pieces, and the bathroom is where you would expect it to be—off the hallway. Dinner is served on weekends in the small pleasant dining room, and it is delicious. Much of the makings come directly off the farm, from the vegetable garden and the livestock, and other items result from trading with neighbors in the area.

The remote setting of the inn gives visitors a chance to catch up on some unstructured back-to-nature activites—picnicking in the rolling grassy hills, bicycling on the Coast Road and evening walks along the old dirt lanes. Best of all are the salt air aromas and the sound of lapping waves from the beach just across the highway. During my visit, fishermen were busily combing the surf with their nets, looking obligingly picturesque.

This rural stretch of countryside hasn't always been so peaceful. There was a fair-sized town around here in the logging days, when lumber mills and flourishing communities seemed to spring up at the mouth of every creek. The town of Dehaven had a livery stable, several saloons, a dancehall, many houses and businesses, and a narrow-gauge railroad that carried logs down to the millpond. When the forests played out, the activity diminished and time

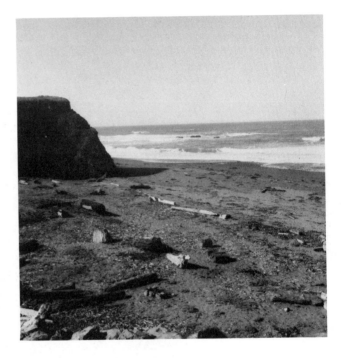

erased everything except the old farmhouse and a couple of cottages. Of such remnants country inns are made.

Dehaven Valley Farm, Westport 95488. (707) 964-2931. Seventeen miles north of Fort Bragg on Highway 1 (2 miles north of the town of Westport). Lodging includes continental breakfast; moderate to expensive. Eight rooms with community bath. Dinner served to guests and the public on Friday and Saturday nights. Reservations required. Ocean beaches nearby. Fishing, hiking, biking.

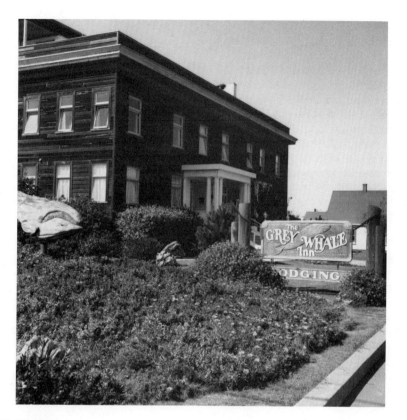

GREY WHALE INN

FORT BRAGG

"The Old Redwood Coast Hospital" has been a landmark on Fort Bragg's Main Street for as long as anyone can remember. It's a relic from the early days of the Union Lumber Company, the town's dominant industry and the center of the local economy. The sprawling mill, now under new ownership, occupies the site of the original military post built in 1857 on the Mendocino Indian Reservation. The post had already been abandoned when C. R. Johnson founded the town, laid out its first streets, and set up his lumber mill on the site.

Johnson was known for his generosity toward the millworkers and their families. His utmost attention was devoted to their safety and welfare. Around 1915, he built the sturdy, all-redwood hospital to handle the medical needs of the company employees. Periodic physical examinations kept the workers in first-rate physical condition for their strenuous jobs in the mill. The hospital changed owners a number of times, but it remained in use as a medical facility until 1972, when the new district hospital was completed. When moving day rolled around, the owners locked the doors for the last time, and an era came to an end.

A short time later, the grey, weathered building with its inviting white entrances was offered for sale. John and Collette Bailey have taken on the task of adapting the stately landmark to its new use as a country inn. The result is first class accommodations for Fort Bragg's visitors.

I would never have guessed that the old building had been anything but a hotel, since its conversion was handled so nicely. I wasn't aware of the building's former function until I was shown the one remaining wheelchair ramp from the series that once connected the floors. The steep inclines didn't work very well for guests struggling to the second floor with armloads of baggage, so the ramps were replaced with handsome redwood stairs, handcrafted by local artisans.

Considerable ingenuity was mixed in with the hard work of refurbishing the rooms. When the former tenants moved out, all of the antiquated equipment was left behind. The old surgical lights were polished to look as good as new and installed as unique lighting fixtures in the cozily furnished guest rooms. The hospital's operating and recovery rooms were turned into charming and spacious suites. The solarium, which rises above the roof, was a sun room for convalescing patients in early days, but it has since been divided into a couple of nifty penthouse rooms with outside decks. The ocean is in sight from these decks, and if you bring binoculars during the migratory season, you may spot one of the grey whales for which the inn is named.

Architecturally, the building is still much as it was in the beginning, except for an addition that was made around 1935. The greatest change was made only a few years ago. Until then the hospital had always been painted entirely white, and it had a very "clincal" appearance. But for maintenance purposes, the siding was replaced with natural redwood which has weathered to a beautiful shade of grey.

The historic setting makes the inn a fine night's lodging for north coast explorers, and especially for railroad buffs making the trip over to Willits and back on the California Western Railroad, better known as the "Skunk." The Fort Bragg depot and the center of town are only two blocks away.

Grey Whale Inn, 615 North Main Street, Fort Bragg 95437. (707) 964-0640. Lodging only; includes continental breakfast; moderate. 13 rooms with private baths; four with kitchens. One room has a bath equipped for handicapped guests. Ramp access to first floor. Billiard table, laundry, rooftop sundeck. Two blocks to restaurants, Skunk depot, lumber-mill tours, and company museum. Scenic Noyo Harbor has good seafood restaurants and fishing charters. Mendocino 10 miles south, ocean beaches, tennis courts, botanical gardens. Paul Bunyan Days in September.

BLUE ROSE INN

FORT BRAGG

A charming little inn sits right on Main Street in Fort Bragg, only a couple of blocks from downtown. This converted home, with clapboard siding and fish-scale shingles, was built entirely of redwood around the turn of the century. A white picket fence surrounds the front yard. The gate, under a latticed arch, leads to an inn of pleasant delights.

The interior is a very homey environment created by Al and Anne Samas. Every room shows their tasteful use of stained glass, brass fixtures, fine fabrics and the careful placement of a nice antique collection. There are numerous innovative touches that will intrigue guests. One wall beside the stairs is papered with real sycamore leaves. A large decorative laundry wringer from the old Elk Hotel serves as a unique conversation piece. The newly crafted redwood ceilings give additional warmth and richness to the already charming rooms.

Six guest rooms are furnished in different styles, some simply, others with very classy bedroom pieces. The rooms on the second floor, including the sitting area, all have oddly shaped ceilings formed by the slopes of the roof, making the spaces all the more interesting.

A hearty traditional breakfast is the only meal served. Lunch and dinner can be enjoyed at fine restaurants within walking distance or at Noyo Harbor.

Behind the house is a garden available to guests for sunning or sitting. A raised wooden boardwalk provides a pathway to the cleverly restored innkeepers' house out back: it was once a garage where workers from the lumber mill repaired engines.

Al Samas's hobby is finding and refurbishing unusual antiques that he picks up around the state. A well-worn old baby buggy was waiting its turn at restoration during my visit. No doubt many more of these relics will be displayed at the inn in the future.

Blue Rose Inn, 520 North Main Street, Fort Bragg 95437. (707) 964-3477. Just north of the downtown business section. Lodging includes breakfast for guests only; moderate. Six rooms, four with private baths; all rooms have washbasins. Skunk Train depot (one block), lumber mill tour, Mendocino Coast Botanical Gardens, scenic Noyo Harbor, beaches nearby. A fine dinner house simply called The Restaurant is only a few doors away.

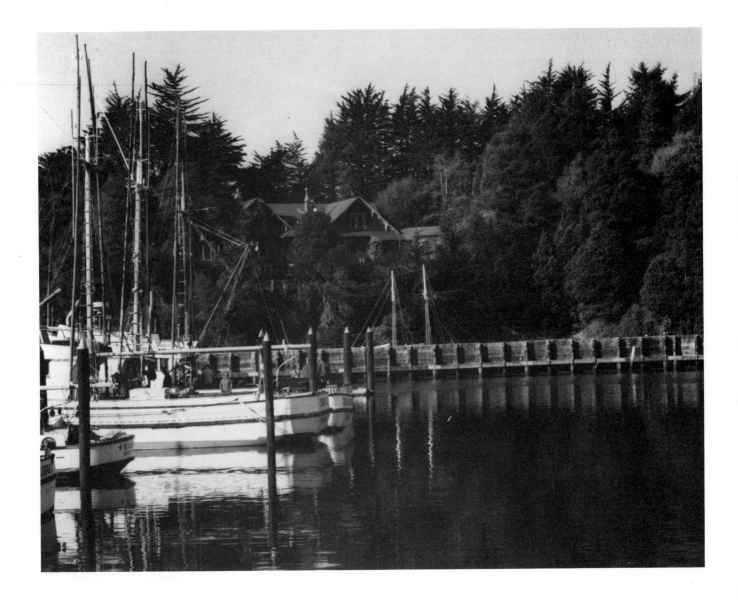

CASA DEL NOYO

FORT BRAGG

From the road leading down into Noyo Harbor, I took the narrow lane that branched left through the trees and along the top of the cliff. The sign stretched over the roadway at the entrance to the overflow parking area read "Casa del Noyo," and gave the feeling of entering the grounds of an age-old resort nestled in the woods.

The harbor below has long been a favorite of mine. Noyo is a thriving fishing village and one of the most picturesque on the West coast. The sight of the boat hands carrying out their daily routines, and the sounds and smells of processing the day's catch, are intriguing.

On the cliff above the harbor sits Casa del Noyo in its secluded yet commanding site. It's a fortunate location for country-inn goers. There are views from each room, some toward the boatworks where hulls are being constructed, others upriver to where hundreds of boats are moored in the basin.

The rustic shingled building with twin gables had its beginning back in 1868 when a large lumber mill was going full blast at the mouth of the river. An executive with the mill built the house. It was much smaller then, but was added to and extensively remodeled around 1910 by Harry Holmes, the mill's Superintendent of Woods.

One great benefit of the remodeling was the beautiful board-and-batten paneling that was used on walls and ceilings throughout the inn. The paneling was installed by skilled Scandinavian boatwrights working as carpenters. Light reflecting off the wood produces a warm glow that gives a wonderful ambience to the rooms.

There are four comfortable bedrooms downstairs and five on the second floor. One has two queen-sized beds spotlighted by a skylight overhead. It has a dark, snug decor and print curtains over the windows. In contrast, the room across the hall is long and spacious with lots of light from several windows that overlook the river. It has a king-sized bed and a writing table, rocker and antique dresser.

Each room has the luxury of a private bath. Some have vintage claw-foot bathtubs and pedestal lavatories with brass fixtures.

A continental breakfast is served each morning, usually on the long wooden deck where sunshine filters through the cypress trees. It's a magnificent location for lingering over steaming coffee and fresh pastries while enjoying the atmosphere of the bustling docks.

Casa del Noyo is a romantic place in every respect. The activity around the inn is unique, from early dawn when the fishing fleet heads out into the morning mist, until the sun sets behind Noyo Bridge. It's a pleasure to discover an inn amid such scenic surroundings.

Casa del Noyo, 500 Casa del Noyo Drive, Fort Bragg 95437. (707) 964-9991. At the north end of Noyo Bridge, follow North Harbor Drive to the inn. Lodging includes continental breakfast for guests only; moderate. Nine rooms with private baths; three with fireplaces. Party boats, lumber mill tour, logging museum, Skunk Train, state parks. Another beautiful shingle-style house in the center of town was formerly a guest house for the lumber mill and is currently being restored as a visitor's center.

JOSHUA GRINDLE INN

MENDOCINO

Mendocino's architecture is so reminiscent of quaint New England villages that moviemakers often pass its townscape for that of East Coast settings. Adding visual delight to this authentic stage set is the Joshua Grindle Inn. This Italianate cottage sits on a knoll behind the town, its large front yard surrounded by a white picket fence. The porch columns are gracefully capped by intricately cut-out brackets, adding a lacy texture to the traditional house form.

The inn was named for its builder, Joshua Grindle. Mr. Grindle was enticed to the Mendocino coast by the properous lumber industry. He worked for the mill at Big River as a raftsman for several years before indulging his interest in the banking business. In 1905 he helped organize the Mendocino Bank of Commerce.

The Grindle house was built in 1879. Bill and Gwen Jacobson, the innkeepers, are only the third owners in the long history of the house, which consequently has seen little change. The house has many fine features of nineteenth-century craftsmanship. The dark wood of the carved stair-railings adds a rich and elegant touch. Several door frames still show the early art of "graining," where the appearance of wood grain was actually painted onto the wood. English-made tiles around one of the fireplace openings are hand-painted with illustrations from Aesop's Fables. All guest rooms have a name: Library, Grindle, Nautical, Cypress and Master. The decor of each complements the name, and the furnishings are nice New England-style antiques from the Jacobsons' collection. The dining room has a long table where guests can chat while partaking of a continental breakfast of homemade bread, fresh fruit, eggs, and coffee or tea.

In the parlor, a backgammon board awaits players in the small glass-enclosed bay that projects from the room. A decanter of sherry and a bowl of fresh fruit on the chest come with the compliments of the inn.

The Joshua Grindle is only a short walk from shops, galleries, restaurants and all the scenic amenities of this historic lumber town. Mendocino is best experienced on foot and every opportunity should be taken to stroll its streets and lanes.

Joshua Grindle Inn, 44800 Little Lake, Mendocino 95460. Mailing address: P.O. Box 647. (707) 937-4143. Lodging includes breakfast for guests only; moderate. Five rooms, two with fireplaces, each with private bath. Biking, beach walking, State Parks.

MacCALLUM HOUSE

MENDOCINO

I didn't know what to expect as I entered MacCallum House. I had photographed the building many times during my previous visits to Mendocino, before the old Victorian house became an inn. The gingerbread-

like Gothic Revival exterior makes this house the most distinctive of all the local buildings and a credit to the town's unique character.

The house originally belonged to Daisy Mac-Callum, the grand dame of Mendocino's past. Her father, William Kelley, presented the fine new house to Daisy and Alexander MacCallum as a wedding present, in keeping with traditional customs of the time. The couple moved into the house in 1882, but didn't live there long before they relocated to Glen Blair where Alexander managed the lumber mill for his uncle, Captain Samuel Blair. Daisy had little affection for the drizzling winter rains of the north coast and soon moved to San Francisco where she lived for the most part in her aunt's beautiful mansion. When Captain Blair died, Alex moved the family to San Francisco and looked after the company's business there.

Alexander MacCallum died in 1908, and Daisy returned to Mendocino to live in her house. She kept busy enlarging the residence, pursuing her interests in botany and horticulture, collecting wildflowers and Indian baskets, and teaching and traveling. Hers was a long and well-spent life. She died in 1953 at the age of 94.

The affluence of the Victorian era is evident from the moment you enter this carpenter's dream, which is still as sturdy and sound as it ever was. The downstairs living room and parlor serve as the inn's dining room, and the rich woodpanelled walls and cobblestone fireplace make an impressive backdrop for the bright blue tablecloths. Daisy's diverse library of books still sits on the shelves.

I was struck by the good feelings that emanated from the mellowed interior and its warm inviting spaces. And the cozy upstairs bedrooms were converted so nicely into lodging rooms. The guests' quarters, which include some oddly shaped attic rooms, are filled with the heirloom furnishings that have always been a part of the house. Small parlors are located here and there where guests can just sit or rest tired feet after touring the streets of Mendocino. My favorite space is the long narrow hideaway in the attic, tucked under the roof and partially papered with nostalgic rotogravure sections from newspapers of the 1920s.

Besides the rooms in the house, there are several other accommodations scattered around the grounds. The little dollhouse structure in the side yard is a guest cottage. The old barn, greenhouse and watertower have also been turned into unusual and distinctive rooms and suites.

Bill and Sue Norris, the owners of MacCallum House, have taken great care to assure that necessary changes were compatible with the historic interior. The Grey Whale Bar was fitted into the first floor and decorated with superb artwork done by local artists. The glassed-in veranda is a bright, sunny spot for afternoon tea. The dining room offers excellent meals by the glow of kerosene lamps, and at times some of Daisy's own recipes are included in the menu.

At the close of my visit, I stopped for a last look at the beautiful eye-catching whale sculpture in the front yard. Its creator is Byrd Baker, Mendocino's leading crusader for stopping the senseless slaughter of whales. The piece is a proper tribute to MacCallum House, for it symbolizes the strong sensitivity of the townspeople in preserving the good things that enrich our lives.

MacCallum House, 740 Albion Street, Mendocino 95460. (707) 937-0289. Lodging on the European plan; moderate to expensive. Twenty rooms, some with private bath. Dining room is open to the public for lunch, dinner and brunch on weekends. The Grey Whale Bar is also open to the public. Russian Gulch State Park, spectaclar cliffs and beaches, fishing, skindiving, beachcombing, hiking nearby. Art galleries and shops, unique crafts in town.

MENDOCINO HOTEL

MENDOCINO

Once a number of hotels were scattered along Mendocino's Main Street. In those days the easiest way to reach the town was by sea, and the Main Street hostelries were readily accessible to travelers arriving by sailing vessels and passenger steamers. By the turn of the century, schooners from all over the world were docking at the busy lumber port, and carriages from each of the hotels went to pick up their share of the incoming passengers.

Ben Beaver was one of the enterprising souls in town. He bought an old house in 1877, moved it back from the street, and built an addition onto the front. In 1878 Beaver opened the "Temperance House" for loggers. His brother, Samuel, joined him in the business, and as the hotel became more successful it was enlarged, and a new false front tied the two sections together. The new front was the handiwork of J. D. Johnson, who built the MacCallum House and other beautiful residences around town. The brothers operated the popular hostelry for twenty-six years as the Central Hotel. Since then the old weathered sign has read simply "Mendocino Hotel."

In the past few years a lot of changes have taken place. Robert Peterson, a retired "Jack-in-the-Box" executive, bought the hotel and rebuilt practically everything behind the historic façade. The interior was enlarged and a Victorian atmosphere was recreated by contemporary craftsmen in a style that would have made the Victorian builders envious. The elegant touch is everywhere—in the rich, tasteful fabrics and wallpaper, the carved-wood panels, the cut-glass screens, and the stained-glass canopies and transoms. Mr. Peterson's amazing collection of period-piece antiques are scattered throughout the guest rooms, dining room and parlors. Even the staff is dressed in Victorian attire.

The hotel is one of the town's best for meals. Diners have the choice of sitting inside in the fancy dining room or outside in the arbor-like setting. On my visit, the coastal village atmosphere prompted me to order the poached salmon, and I don't recall ever having tasted any that could beat it. The kitchen's bakery turns out its own fresh-baked aromatic breads. Overnight guests are treated to a continental breakfast made up of an assortment of these nut and fruit breads, along with fresh orange juice or coffee.

The best lodging rooms have an excellent view of Mendocino Bay, and some have French doors opening onto a long balcony across the side of the building. In spite of all the luxury, several rooms don't have private baths, but nice white robes are waiting in the wooden wardrobes for those who have to make the trip across the hall.

You can bet that the original owners had nothing so extravagant in mind for the burly loggers who frequented the premises. But the clientele has changed quite a bit since the old days, and the hotel is merely keeping pace.

Mendocino Hotel, 45080 Main Street, Mendocino 95460. (707) 937-0511. Lodging includes breakfast for guests only; moderate. Twenty-four rooms, most with private baths. Dining room serving lunch and dinner, enclosed dining terrace, and the bar are open to the public. Management specifically prohibits pets. Quaint New England-style village; art galleries and specialty shops.

MENDOCINO VILLAGE INN

MENDOCINO

So many doctors have lived in this two-story white residence on Main Street that it is commonly referred to as "the doctors' house." Historically, though, it is known as the McCornack House. William McCornack built the house in 1882, and was the first doctor to live here. It seems that nearly all the pioneers of early Mendocino had some connection with the lumber industry, and Dr. McCornack was no exception. A few years after building the house, he purchased land north of Fort Bragg and built a chute for shipping wood ties and tanbark.

Over the years the house was lived in by Doctors Milliken, Moore and Peirsol. Now it is a charming inn and typical of the quaint lodging found in Mendocino. The New England façade hides behind lush foliage and a white picket fence. The gambrel-style roof and dormer windows are barely visible from the street.

The guest accommodations are absolutely fascinating, from the large, elegant suite on the first floor to the small, cozy attic rooms fitted under the sloping roof rafters. Some have parlors, fireplaces, bathrooms and ocean views. All have beautiful antique furnishings and a lot of charm.

The inn serves no meals, but the town is noted for many interesting restaurants. The Sea Gull Inn, for example, serves from morning until evening. Both MacCallum House and the Mendocino Hotel are excellent choices for dinner. A smaller and more intimate treat is Cafe Beaujolais. This fine French restaurant is very intimate—it has just a handful of tables. It is located on Ukiah Street, just a couple of blocks behind the Mendocino Village Inn. Every course is distinctive, and there is even a choice of coffee blends. Because of the restaurant's size, dinner reservations are a necessity.

Mendocino Village Inn, Main Street, Mendocino 95460. (707) 937-0246. Lodging only; inexpensive to moderate. Three rooms with private bath, 9 rooms without. Shops and restaurants nearby. Town has seacoast environment; close to beaches, water sports facilities.

GLENDEVEN

LITTLE RIVER

Farmhouses have always intrigued me, particularly the handsome ones that sit so elegantly in their rural surroundings. My interest is greatly satisfied each time I drive along the Mendocino coast, where some of the most picturesque are to be found. One of these finely preserved specimens of rural life is now called Glendeven. It is a classic, its noble forms covered with clapboard siding and beautifully painted to blend with the forest.

Isaiah Stevens built the house for his wife and family. They arrived in Little River in 1864 after a long trip by sea from Maine. By 1867 the house was complete, and the sturdy structure was home to various members of the Stevens family until the 1930s. Isaiah Stevens held jobs as chief clerk at the local lumber mill and as Little River's first postmaster. He also found time to develop the farm complex as a renowned facility for the breeding of fine livestock. The large red barn behind the house was a part of the complex. It is now being restored by the owners as their living quarters.

Glendeven is the venture of Jan and Janet DeVries, a young couple from Portland. They had previously lived and worked in the Mendocino area and had fond memories of the farmhouse through friendship with the previous owners. When the house was offered for sale recently, they couldn't resist the opportunity to become innkeepers.

The old farmhouse is perfect as a country inn, sitting under large cypress trees at the edge of the forest. Guests have the use of the large solarium-like living room and its cozy fireplace. There are six guest rooms in all. The most exciting is the Garret Room on the top floor by itself. It has the best view of the ocean and the surrounding countryside. All of the guest rooms are very appealing and furnished with wood or brass bedsteads, fine artwork on the walls, and an abundance of potted plants.

Janet said that she hoped guests looking for a luxurious time on the north coast would not be disappointed by Glendeven's modest accommodations. But no one should feel slighted here. The house and the DeVrieses show such warmth that the experience adds immeasurably to my concept of a perfect Mendocino weekend.

Glendeven, 8221 North Highway 1, Little River 95456. (707) 937-0083. Two miles south of Mendocino on the east side of Hwy. 1. Lodging includes continental breakfast for guests only; moderate. Six rooms, two with private baths. Beaches within walking distance; biking, hiking in Van Damme State Park, golf and tennis nearby. Excellent restaurants at Ledford House, Little River Inn, Heritage House.

LITTLE RIVER INN

LITTLE RIVER

The old main house at the Little River Inn is as pretty as a New England picture. And rightly so. Its builder was Silas Coombs who, like many other settlers in the area, was attracted to the California frontier from his home in Maine. He arrived here in 1857.

Coomb's trip westward through Panama was hair-raising. Riots were occurring between the natives and the immigrants, and in the turmoil Coombs lost everything except the clothes on his back. After arriving in San Francisco, he immediately headed north to the forests around Albion to find whatever work was available in the booming lumber industry. He worked in the mill and woods for a salary and eventually formed a partnership with a close friend, whereby they contracted to furnish the mill with logs. Success followed from there, and Silas Coombs became a rich man. He owned several mills at Little River and a number of shipping schooners.

Coombs went home to Maine in 1864 and married Margaret Boyd, and the couple returned to Little River to live in the mansion that he had begun. It was an elegant home commensurate with his wealth, having conservatories, parlors, verandas, and the character of the farmhouses Coombs had known so well back home.

Little River Inn wouldn't be the unique lodging it is without the old house. The picturesque façade makes this one of the most beautiful structures on the California coast. Although there are many newer units in the cottages around the grounds, I found that the real charm is in the inn: at the top of the carpeted stairs in the six attic rooms, and especially in those that face the ocean. Some interesting oil landscapes decorate the wood-panelled walls, but the ocean landscape through the white shuttered window is a view to beat all views. On a clear day you can spot the fishing fleet, or even whales during the migratory season. To lie in bed at night and listen to the soothing sound of the distant surf is to know the true atmosphere of the north coast.

The ground floor spaces have been rearranged to accommodate the office, a spacious bar that keeps long hours, and the wallpapered dining room. Along with homemade breads and soups, the dinner menu includes such coastal seafood specialties as fresh filets of cod and sole, salmon, abalone and fried oysters. Steaks are a specialty also. At one end of the dining room is a gigantic picture window with a dramatic view of lush ferns and flowering shrubbery.

Just down the road and around the bend is Van Damme State Park. This narrow strip of land reaches from the ocean tidepools back into the dense forest of second-growth redwoods, fern canyons and pygmy forests.

Little River Inn, Little River 95456. (707) 937-5942. Three miles south of Mendocino on Highway 1. Open all year. Lodging on the European plan; moderate. Six attic rooms with private baths; other modern units available. Dining room serves all meals to the public. A 9-hole golf course on the grounds. Ocean beaches, biking, hiking and Mendocino shops nearby.

HERITAGE HOUSE

LITTLE RIVER

It's hard to imagine a more spectacular location for an inn than the north coast setting of Heritage House. The rambling resort stretches along the brink of a rugged, craggy cove, sculptured over the centuries by the pounding surf. Whether peaceful or raging, the wave action of the cove and the intriguing moods of the weather against the forest landscape are a couple of reasons why guests return time and again to this captivating retreat. Another is the warm hospitality of the Dennens, who have created a country inn around the handsome old farmhouse that serves as its headquarters.

The farmhouse was built in 1877 by Wilder Pullen and a relative, John Dennen, who was the present innkeeper's grandfather. In those days, houses were strictly handmade, and the cutting, hauling and splitting of timbers was accomplished by neighbors who gathered for the traditional "house-raising." Many of the Little River pioneers came from Maine, and this old farmhouse reflects characteristics of the buildings they knew best. Wilder Pullen and his wife Etta lived on their 160-acre claim for thirty-six years and operated a landing below the house from which redwood ties, posts and timbers were shipped to such boom towns as San Francisco and Eureka.

But lumber wasn't the only product shipped at Pullen's Landing. A healthy market for laborers developed on the new frontier, and boatloads of Oriental workers were smuggled into the cove. Later, during the early thirties, bootlegging activities led "Baby Face" Nelson to use the by then abandoned farmhouse as a hideout, but he skipped before the Prohibition Agents closed in.

The barns and outbuildings of the farm are long gone, but in their place are several guest cottages. I was amazed when I first discovered how well the newer buildings blended into the landscape— what I thought was a grassy knoll turned out to be the sod roof of a cottage tucked into an embankment. Other buildings here, of an older vintage, once sat in various parts of the county until they were dismantled and brought to the site: for instance, the hundred-year-old "Apple House," attached to the inn, and the old wooden water tower with its unique accommodations.

Almost every unit has an ocean view, and some have fireplaces or stoves for that real country-inn feeling. Each cottage has a name, such as School-house, Stable or Country Store, and the decor and furnishings reflect the name. A few guest rooms are upstairs in the Apple House and furnished with handsome period pieces. Many of the antiques have a history of their own.

I liked strolling about the grounds after beginning the day by choosing from the buffet-breakfast offerings of fresh fruit, assorted juices, and oatmeal topped with butter and brown sugar. The waitress brings the special-order items such as eggs, bacon and hotcakes. My table by the window had its own toaster, a marvelous convenience for breakfasters who like their toast well-done.

Down the hill near the duckpond, several friendly ducks rushed forward in search of attention or a handout. The invigorating blend of warm sun and salt air invited an early-morning walk along the cliff, high above the lapping waves.

For the rest of the day, plenty of diversions are to be found in the town of Mendocino (five miles to the north), along the beach or among the giant red-woods and pygmy forests. Dinner at the inn features an ever-changing fare which has gained much acclaim for its distinctive courses.

Heritage House is a refuge from all city pressures—a fine place to be alone or to meet friends, whichever the mood compels. It's a classy place, and luxury is part of its appeal. The service, the privacy, the high quality of the food and the hospitality of the Dennens make a stay there a most remarkable experience.

Heritage House, Little River 95456. (707) 937-5885. Five miles south of Mendocino on Highway 1. Closed December and January. Lodging on the modified American plan includes breakfast and dinner; moderate to expensive. Forty-six accommodations, all with private baths. Dining room open to the public with reservations. Ocean beaches, Van Damme State Park and Mendocino village are close by.

HARBOR HOUSE

ELK

My architectural sensibilities had a field day when I entered the big living room at Harbor House. The rich, redwood-panelled walls and ceiling combine to form a very impressive room. Clearly the place was designed to make a strong impression.

In 1916, Mr. Goodyear decided that the Goodyear Lumber Company should have a spectacular guest house to accommodate important eastern contacts during their visits to the mill. He borrowed his concept for the building from the Redwood Model Home designed by Louis Christian Mullgardt and exhibited at the 1915 Panama-Pacific Exposition in

San Francisco. The basic design of the home was enlarged and embellished to suit Mr. Goodyear's grandiose plans and was constructed by the finest craftsmen. Every stick of trim in the beautiful living room was hand-shaped and carefully fitted; then it was rubbed to a fine sheen with hot beeswax to preserve the color and quality of the wood.

As an inn, the old building remains as sumptuous as ever. Patricia Corcoran, the innkeeper, is an exuberant woman who traded home and career in a suburban town for the more leisurely way of life on the north coast. The revitalization of the house is an ongoing experience, and the Edwardian atmosphere associated with its era of construction is becoming more and more evident.

There are five guest rooms in the inn, and off to the side of the house are four cottages built in the 1920s. Much of the ambience of the rooms comes from the Franklin stoves and fireplaces, the patterned wallpaper, the antique beds of wood and brass and the ever-present seascape.

A winding footpath leads downhill to the inn's private beach. Here guests have a closeup view of the ocean pounding into the wave-carved tunnels. Farther up the creek that runs down to the sea is a small waterfall which spills into a lush grotto-like pool.

From the sundeck of Harbor House guests can enjoy a magnificent view across the treetops to the cove, a very active place during the company's existence. A collection of historic photos on the wall of the dining room gives a fair indication of the elaborate lumbering operations that took place around here. The stories surrounding the ships, their captains and their perilous ventures into the hazardous cove are quite fascinating.

The real gregariousness takes place at dinner-time, when everyone gathers to enjoy the fine home-

made feasts concocted in the kitchen. Pat Corcoran and her helpers prepare some superb meals for their guests, who are allowed a leisurely pace of dining and socializing.

Solitude and privacy are well respected at this traditional country inn, but there's no lack of companionship if you desire it. It's the sort of place where you'll arrive as strangers, but leave having made a dozen new friends.

Harbor House, P.O. Box 167, Elk 95432. (707) 877-3203. South of Mendocino 17 miles on Highway 1. Lodging, on the modified American plan, includes breakfast and dinner for guests only; moderate to expensive. Nine rooms and cottages, all with private baths. Biking, fishing, skindiving, beach rambling nearby.

ELK COVE INN

ELK

The sign on the old wooden water tower welcomes you to Elk Cove Inn. The charming little house is very French in appearance and sits below the roadway on a bluff overlooking the vast Pacific. It was built in the 1880s by the L. E. White Lumber Company and served as the company house. Just downhill are traces of the foundations from the huge lumber mill that operated between 1890 and 1929. The mill was noted for the incredible system of chutes and inclines reaching from rock to rock that carried the lumber several hundred yards offshore to waiting schooners.

Now that Elk's days as a lumber port are history, the sleepy little town is gaining new fame for its inns and the peaceful environment they offer. Michael and Hildrun-Uta Boynoff are the innkeepers at the Elk Cove. In addition to their active participation in local civic causes, they find time to provide the satisfying country inn experience so eagerly sought by visitors to the north coast.

The inn consists of two guest rooms in the main house, a cottage out back and several rooms in an annex about half a mile up the road on the opposite side of town. The annex is another old residence, called Sandpiper House, built as guest quarters for the lumber company's visitors sometime between 1917 and 1920. Most of the inn's guests will find themselves quartered here, where the area in front of the fireplace in the big redwood-beamed living room is a congenial gathering spot. A trail behind Sandpiper House leads to a sheltered beach, and you can wander along the cove behind the main house to explore the old mill site and enjoy the sounds and smells of the ocean sprays.

Breakfast and dinner are also part of the experience—good home-style cooking where everything is made from scratch. Dinner is a full evening's affair at the inn and features some of Mrs. Boynoff's favorite German and French recipes, as well as her home-baked bread. Michael Boynoff is the salad chef, tossing fresh garden vegetables with garlic, dill and Parmesan dressings. Black bean or leek and potato soups are often served prior to the entree and vegetables. A dessert such as five-layer torte, and exotic coffee from freshly ground beans, culminate the feast.

The days of fresh-cut timber spilling out of the mouth of Greenwood Creek are gone, but this historic setting offers a fine north coast experience in the company of two very friendly people.

Elk Cove Inn, P.O. Box 367, Elk 95432. (707) 877-3321. Seventeen miles south of Mendocino on Highway 1. Lodging on the modified American plan includes dinner and breakfast for guests; moderate to expensive. Meals served Friday through Sunday. Dinner served to the public by reservation only. Rooms in two old houses and one cottage. Fishing, biking, ocean beaches, skindiving close by.

OLD MILANO HOTEL

GUALALA

Perched on a cliff overlooking the ocean, a most incredible hotel sits hidden behind the trees just north of Gualala. It has been there since 1905, serving first as a hotel and then as a private residence. The cycle

has been completed, for the hotel is again a hotel. This time its back is to the highway; in earlier days the wagon road passed in front, as did the railroad that hauled lumber south along the coast from Mendocino.

The Old Milano is quite remarkable for its romantic location, its extensive restoration, and the history that has earned it a place in the National Register of Historic Places. An Italian family built the structure when Gualala was a busy logging town, and the ground floor was outfitted as a saloon. An old photograph in the parlor shows a group of patrons gathered outside on the porch to toast the new enterprise.

The present-day innkeepers are just as remarkable as the hotel. Bruce and Theodora McBroom traded Hollywood glamor for a more relaxing place in the country. He is a photographer, and some of the most famous personalities in the entertainment world have posed before his camera. She is a costume designer, with fashions from such films as *Bonnie and Clyde* among her credits.

Their Hollywood success has been matched by their success in reviving the hotel as a country inn. Bruce did the backbreaking work of tearing away the modernized finishes, sanding floors, restoring the board ceilings, and generally putting the hotel back together as it once was. Theodora applied all of her design talent to recreate Victorianism at its best. Everything—Morris wallpapers, impressive antiques, original paintings, vintage knick-knacks—blends perfectly to create elegant guest rooms. Fresh cut flowers from the garden are placed throughout the hotel. Most rooms have a view of the spectacular coastline where pounding waves crash against Castle Rock in the cove below. The inn is a fabulous vantage point for watching the changing moods of the weather, from drifting fogs and winter storms to beautiful sunny days.

Passersby can't help but be intrigued or curious about the Old Milano, and they stop by just to get a glimpse of the rooms and wander around the grounds. Occasionally "high teas" are held on Sunday afternoons on the lawn-covered bluff.

In spite of all the restoration work that has been done, the McBrooms are not finished. They

have elaborate projects planned for the grounds around the hotel and hope to rebuild the second floor balcony that once wrapped around three sides. It's only a matter of time before the Old Milano regains its appearance of 1905.

Old Milano Hotel, 38300 Highway 1, Gualala 95445. Mailing address: P.O. Box 385. (707) 884-3256. Lodging includes continental breakfast for guests only; moderate to expensive. Six rooms share two luxurious baths. Closed January through March. Ocean beaches, backroads, Gualala Point Country Park, biking. St. Orres Inn, 2 miles north of Gualala, offers a fine dining experience for lunch and dinner.

The Wine Country

THE WINE COUNTRY

A maze of scenic backroads criss-crosses the pastoral countryside of Napa and Sonoma counties. The landscape of vineyards, orchards, dairy farms and rolling hills is also dotted with such colorful historical sites as the Petaluma Adobe at Petaluma, General Vallejo's home at Sonoma and the Old Bale Mill north of St. Helena.

The abundant and picturesque wineries are as famous for their beauty as they are for their wine. Some date back to the 1850s and have given the region its claim to fame. At St. Helena a beautiful Gothic mansion serves as a tasting room at the Beringer Brothers Winery. Nearby, the Christian Brothers Winery occupies a huge rambling stone structure. Inglenook Winery sits back from the highway at Rutherford. The façade is covered with Boston ivy that turns a brilliant red in autumn. Buena Vista, the oldest of the wineries, is just outside of Sonoma in a shady glen surrounded by picnic tables.

For the curious who want to see how wine is made, September and October are the height of the harvest season, when the grape crushing takes place and the aroma of fermenting wine permeates the air. Many wineries are open throughout the year and offer tours through the jungles of wooden storage casks, which are sometimes kept underground in limestone caves. The popular wine-tasting rooms are open all year.

The climate that is so good for growing grapes is generous to tourists also. Summer daytime temperatures range from the seventies into the nineties, but nights are cool and comfortable. Winters are normally mild, and the thermometer seldom falls below freezing. There is a rainy season during the winter months, but even rain can't spoil a winery tour.

The added attractions of the wine country are the many farms, ranches and country craftsmen who sell their products directly to the consumer at bargain prices. Families headed home from a weekend outing can stop at these rural outlets and stock up on apple cider, jams, nuts, fresh vegetables, smoked meats, Christmas trees—almost anything rural, from birdhouses to pumpkins. To get a map, send a long, stamped, self-addressed envelope to *Sonoma County Farm Trails*, Box 6043, Santa Rosa 95406.

CHALET BERNENSIS

ST. HELENA

Some of the most impressive nineteenth-century architecture in the Napa Valley is found in and around the historic town of St. Helena. Numerous storefronts along Main Street, particularly 1331 Main, present fine examples of stone masonry construction and fanciful variations of Queen Anne façades. Just north of town are the magnificent winery buildings at Christian Brothers, Beringer and Charles Krug. The vintners left their mark on the Valley not only with their imposing wineries, but also with their beautiful residences.

The legacy is quite evident in one of the wine country's most prestigious inns, Chalet Bernensis. John Thomann built the home in 1884. He was a prominent winemaker who owned the Sutter Home Winery, which is still in operation next door to the inn. The mansion has always been admired in its prominent site on this well traveled route through the wine country. Old photos from the late 1800s show that trolleys and trains passed within yards of the front door, carrying tourists north to soak in the mud baths and mineral waters at Calistoga.

Jack and Essie Doty have created a welcome stop for travelers, complete with an antique shop and gallery. Tourists who seek the inn as a base for explorations have five rooms to choose from on the mansion's upper floor. Each one is furnished with antiques, lace curtains, and handmade quilts on the beds.

Four more rooms are located in a newly constructed water tower that sits beside the house. It was built to duplicate the tower that once occupied the site and matches the detailing of the original very accurately. The rooms are small and cozy, with private baths and old-fashioned decor. One room has a pair of matching twin beds with inlaid wood designs, a rare antique set.

The spacious grounds set the mood for the elegance of the estate. A gravel driveway curves around the lawns of grass and groundcover to the front door, where guests can be dropped off. It's a grand approach for carriages, even horseless ones.

Chalet Bernensis, 225 St. Helena Highway, St. Helena 94574. (707) 963-4423. On the south side of town on Highway 29 (St. Helena Highway). Lodging includes breakfast for guests only; moderate. Five rooms in the inn share two-and-one-half baths; the four water tower rooms have private baths. No smoking, pets, or children. La Belle Helene Restaurant in St. Helena (restored stone hatchery). Wineries, glider flights, good bicycling roads. Old Bale Mill, 3½ miles. Bothe-Napa Valley State Park, 4 miles. Petrified Forest, 12 miles.

INK HOUSE

ST. HELENA

Theron Ink was one of Napa County's prominent landowners, amassing several thousand acres throughout the Valley. In spite of the very large parcels he held, it was on his small, 133-acre plot between Rutherford and St. Helena that he built a handsome Italianate farmhouse encircled by a wide veranda. The property was nothing more than a large duck pond when he bought it in 1878. It wasn't long, though, before he improved the property, putting in miles of underground tiling as an irrigation system and setting out acres of grapevines. By 1886 his winery was producing 150,000 gallons of fine wine annually.

The Clark family bought the Ink House twelve years ago. As a hobby, Mrs. Clark has turned their home into a country inn, partly to keep the large house from feeling empty now that their children are grown, and partly to satisfy the need for more lodging in the area.

The house is exquisite and attracts a great deal of curiosity. It was built over a huge stone cellar which perhaps served as a repository for much of Mr. Ink's wine. Three upstairs rooms are available to guests, each furnished with old-fashioned beds and dressers. A large spacious bathroom, common in old homes such as this, is shared by the three rooms. Each morning a continental breakfast of coffee, juice and nutbread is set out on the long dining table for guests to enjoy at their leisure.

In the future, the Clarks hope to reconstruct the open observatory that once graced the top of the house. It was from this 360-degree vantage point that Theron Ink kept an eye on his workmen in the vineyards.

Ink House, 1575 St. Helena Highway, St. Helena 94574. (707) 963-3890. Three miles south of St. Helena on Highway 29 (St. Helena Highway) at Whitehall Lane. Lodging includes continental breakfast for guests only; moderate. Three rooms share one bath. Closed before and after Christmas. No smoking inside. Restaurants in St. Helena (3 miles) and Yountville (7 miles). Wineries nearby, back roads, Vintage 1870 shops in Yountville.

MAGNOLIA HOTEL

YOUNTVILLE

All the fascinating qualities of the wine country are embodied in the colorful little town of Yountville, which sits squarely in the heart of the Napa Valley vineyards. Historical preservation has a strong foot-hold here and is making the town an inviting place for tourists and day visitors from the Bay Area. Activity is centered around the restoration of the Groezinger Winery buildings, now transformed into a maze of shops, galleries, restaurants and boutiques called Vintage 1870. Nearby, the Yountville depot is alive and useful, and several interesting shops are located in the old railroad cars that were recently added to the scene.

Two beautiful stone buildings have been revived as country inns. One of these is the Magnolia Hotel on Yount Street. It was always a hotel from the time it was built in 1873, but as the town degenerated, so did the hotel. When previous owners discovered the boarded-up building a few years ago, it was so neglected and run down that great foresight was needed to recognize its future potential as a country inn. Two years of blood, sweat and tears made the old relic more charming than it ever was.

The Magnolia wasn't the most respectable place in town in its younger days. Traveling salesmen and shady ladies frequented its upper floors. As could be expected, the sheriff and district attorney did a land-office business in the wine country during Prohibition. Old newspaper accounts tell of the Magnolia Hotel being raided; numerous people were arrested and charged with selling alcoholic beverages.

One of the hotel's more upstanding owners was Frenchman Pierre Guillaume. Monsieur Guillaume was a law-abiding citizen noted for the mineral water he bottled from natural springs on his property at Pope Valley. So remarkable were his talents that his product received an award at the 1915 Panama Exposition in San Francisco. The award now hangs in the foyer of the hotel.

The Magnolia only has seven guest rooms, on the second and third floors. All are impressive, with their beautiful brass, wood, and intricate iron beds against the backdrop of newly exposed brick and stone walls. Overnight guests are treated to a real old-fashioned breakfast, and in each room they find a complimentary decanter of wine—a little reminder of this picturesque grape-growing region. A swimming pool surrounded by lawns and a twelve-foot Jacuzzi are inviting retreats on hot summer days and warm nights.

The proprietors, Bruce and Bonnie Locken, also operate the popular restaurant next door. It is a very small room containing only seven tables and a cozy fireplace. The restaurant has received awards for its superb dinners, and praise from none other than Julia Child. Also stocked in the cellar is an outstanding selection of California wines.

It was plain good fortune that the Napa Valley and its mild climate attracted people who would someday gain immortality as masters of wine production—such greats as Krug, Schram, Beringer, and Martini. It was equally fortunate that they were followed by the skilled European and Chinese immigrants who would find their own place in the Valley's history—as a labor force, constructing handsome rock walls, tunnels, bridges and stone wineries. These skilled laborers were probably responsible for the fine stonework in the Magnolia Hotel.

Magnolia Hotel, 6529 Yount Street, Yountville 94599. (707) 944-2056. Ten miles north of Napa on Highway 29. Lodging includes full breakfast for guests only; expensive. Seven rooms with private baths. Restaurant open to the public for dinner. Close to Vintage 1870 shops, numerous wineries, and interesting back roads.

BURGUNDY HOUSE

YOUNTVILLE

Somehow, it doesn't matter so much that the old stone structure called Burgundy House was once a speakeasy, a school, a bordello, an LSD factory, an antique shop, a residence—you name it. Of all its uses, its present status as a country inn seems most fitting and most fortunate for visitors to the wine country. The building was originally constructed as a winery by Charles Rouvegneau in 1872. Large, beautiful stones were hauled in from the surrounding countryside by Mr. Rouvegneau and his workers and laid up to make walls twenty-two inches thick. This was typical construction for many of the early Napa Valley wineries.

The Keenans, the present owners, first established an antique shop in the ground floor of the building, but one day they were talked into putting up guests in the upper rooms. After that, Burgundy House became so popular as an inn that the shop was moved out and guests now have the run of the place, with six beautiful rooms to choose from. The rooms are particularly nice because they are furnished with fine antique pieces from the Keenan's collection. The rugged stone walls add their own kind of charm. Guests will find a fruit basket and decanter of wine waiting on the bureau, and a pleasant shady patio out back. Breakfast is served around the big table downstairs. The original antique shop was replaced by what you might call the game room, which features a large pool table.

The size of the building, the quiet atmosphere and the quaint appearance make Burgundy House as reminiscent of a European inn as anything you'll find in California. And its wine country setting, with vineyards in all directions, couldn't be more picturesque.

Burgundy House, 6711 Washington St., Yountville 94599. (707) 944-2711. Ten miles north of Napa on Highway 29. Lodging includes continental breakfast; expensive. One room with private bath, five rooms share two baths. Three cottages are nearby, and six additional rooms with patios and private baths are being constructed. Game room, patio. Close to Vintage 1870 shops, numerous wineries and interesting backroads.

WEBBER PLACE

YOUNTVILLE

Not all of Yountville's inns are built of stone. Webber Place is a handsome clapboard house, rusty red in color, with a dainty white picket fence encircling the yard.

Both Webber Place and the street it's on were named for the family that occupied the house around the turn of the century. Mr. Webber was a prominent politician. The house itself is believed to have been built by one Captain John Grigsby. It was originally a much smaller cottage that was moved to its present site sometime before 1900. Additions, such as the dormer over the front porch, were made in the 1920s.

After extensive remodeling, the house is now a country inn. Loren Holti, the proprietor, has gone to great lengths to make the structure inviting and comfortable. In the process, he had the good fortune to find a local craftsman who could duplicate the traditional door and wainscot moldings as well as handfit wood panels into intricate designs on the walls. The old board ceilings had been painted various strange colors over the years. So each wood strip was cleverly taken down, flipped over, and replaced, revealing the natural redwood finish that had been hidden from view. While the floors were being repaired, bundles of old newspapers were found under the floorboards upstairs, perhaps intended as insulation. Several of the front pages, announcing historic events of the 1915 era, were framed and now hang on the walls of the guest rooms.

Guests will find some very interesting accommodations. The Sun Room is aptly named, having large multipaned windows reaching almost to the floor. It is simply furnished with a huge wooden bed, antique dresser and potted palm. The Redwood Room has walls paneled with boards fitted together in geometric designs. The East Room has an iron bedstead and a particularly romantic atmosphere. A huge, old-fashioned bathtub, instead of being closeted away, sits openly on a tiled floor in one end of the spacious room. The walls of the closet in this room were papered with many old newspapers by one of the Webber family members early in the century. The walls have been preserved as they were found.

The Oval Room was undergoing restoration during my visit, but promises to be even more elaborate than the others. It has French doors that open onto an outside deck, a private entrance and a combined bed and bath layout.

In the future, the dining room, where a continental breakfast is served, will open onto a new patio deck. A gazebo will also be erected in the garden, and a watertower structure, of the type that typically sat next to nineteenth-century homes, will be constructed in the side yard.

I'm constantly amazed at how each inn is unique and different, with distinctive touches that set it apart from all the others. Webber Place has its share.

Webber Place, 6610 Webber Street, Yountville 94599. (707) 944-8384. Ten miles north of Napa on State 29. Two blocks from the center of town at Webber and Jefferson streets. Lodging includes a continental breakfast for guests only; moderate. Four rooms, two with private baths. Wineries, Vintage 1870 (winery buildings restored as shops, galleries and restaurants), Magnolia Hotel Restaurant within walking distance (reservations only).

SONOMA HOTEL

SONOMA

Reviving this old hotel and altering its 1950s flophouse character took a lot of work. But the Sonoma Hotel is once again a charming, gracious hostelry, providing the only lodging directly on the plaza in the heart of Sonoma.

The historic plaza is the largest of its kind in California and is ringed with history. The hotel is only a stone's throw from the Mission San Francisco Solano, the Sonoma Barracks, and the Toscano Hotel. The latter has been restored as an historical representation, to show what an unpretentious hotel of the 1850s was like. Across the street from the mission is the Blue Wing Inn, built in the 1840s and now an antique shop. The Blue Wing was one of the first hotels north of San Francisco, and it entertained the famous and infamous alike—Kit Carson and U. S. Grant, as well as the bandit Joaquin Murietta and "Three-Fingered Jack."

The Sonoma Hotel, under other names, had its beginnings in the 1880s as a two-story adobe when the town still had the primitive appearance of a small frontier village. It was a convenient stopping place and a short walk from the depot, where stagecoaches arrived and departed daily. In the 1920s the pioneer hotel was purchased by Sam Sebastiani, one of the Valley's famous winemakers. He did well with his vineyards and invested much of his fortune in the restoration of his newly acquired properties and the building of many new businesses. Sonoma became a modern progressive city thanks to Sebastiani's efforts.

The sawdust has settled now on a new phase in the hotel's history, since the increasing popularity of country inns gave it a new lease on life. In 1974 the aging building was purchased by John and Dorene Musilli, who resurrected it, saved it from its condemned status and proceeded to revive its turn-of-the-century qualities. The work wasn't easy, but the blisters, splinters, and back-breaking labor turned the derelict structure into a handsome European-style inn for visitors exploring the wine country.

The lobby is a bright and inviting space with big windows that look out onto the plaza. The old stone fireplace hasn't worked for some time, but it still adds character to the entry.

The most impressive accommodation in the hotel contains a giant bed which fills much of the room. Its headboard almost touches the ceiling and is one of the most elaborately carved pieces I've seen. This is no ordinary bed. Along with the fancy bureau, it once belonged to General Vallejo's sister and has

generously been loaned to the inn's management by the Sonoma League for Historic Preservation.

All of the other rooms have their own items of furniture that will intrigue lovers of antiques. Most notable are the variety of beds: an elegant brass frame in one room, a rare set of matching twins in another, a sleigh bed in birds-eye maple, a handcarved pair from Austria, some in oak or mahogany, others of iron. The owners have gone to great lengths to assemble a collection of original period pieces representative of the hotel's early furnishings.

The only thing missing from the inn today is the grand balcony that used to stretch across the front and sides of the building. Its deteriorating condition reached a point of no return and it was removed. With it went a favorite front-row seat for the Vintage Festival parade, the highlight of Sonoma County's tribute to the wine industry.

Sonoma Hotel, 110 W. Spain Street, Sonoma 95476. (707) 996-2996. Located on the northwest corner of the plaza. Lodging includes continental breakfast; moderate. Seventeen rooms, five with private bath. Excellent restaurants nearby, historic adobes, numerous wineries, antique shops, interesting back roads. Jack London State Historic Park, 8 miles. Vintage Festival held in September.

WASHOE HOUSE

PETALUMA

Sonoma County is ribboned with scenic, unspoiled back roads, a network I always choose over high-speed freeways. It was on one of these less traveled routes, Stony Point Road, that I stumbled upon the

Washoe House. This historic, pioneer hotel from California's stagecoach days still operates as a busy restaurant and bar.

According to historical documents, the Washoe was built in 1859, making it one of the oldest of the early roadhouses still existing in the state. A sturdy redwood frame pieced together with hand-made square nails and pegs accounts for its longevity.

Even the big jolt of 1906 couldn't bring it down.

One story has it that an Illinois gentleman, on his way west, stopped over at a hotel called Washoe House while passing through Washoe County, Nevada. He was so impressed with the place that when he arrived in California, he erected his own hotel on Stony Point Road and named it after the Nevada inn.

There was a small community here once, with a general store, carriage factory, butcher's shop and post office. Salty drivers drove the daily stages along the dusty pitted roads to this half-way point between Petaluma and Santa Rosa, and stopped to wash the dust out of their throats with a drink at the bar. As a junction for the stage lines, the hotel did a brisk business catering to miners, pioneer businessmen and the troupers of traveling road shows. Like most hotels of early days, Washoe House served the local citizenry well as a social center. Weekly dances in the big ballroom on the second floor attracted young and old from miles around. The legend persists that Ulysses S. Grant gave a speech from the wide balcony across the front. But although he was invited to attend a Petaluma agricultural fair in 1879, there is no evidence that he visited the hotel.

Washoe House is all that's left of the rural village now, and it no longer operates as a hotel, but is a restaurant only. The restaurant is an experience, and the clientele is diverse—sophisticated city types drink at the bar alongside ranchhands, while teenagers dine in prom attire. But the true atmosphere is casual, in keeping with the rustic setting.

The two small dining rooms have a pleasant intimacy, but the tables across from the bar are best for watching the crowd. There is no menu, just a blackboard at the rear of the barroom where the ever-changing specialties of the day are noted. I had broiled salmon served with salad, vegetables and large chunks of french fries, and my dinner was excellent. Other choices were steak, prime rib, chicken and jumbo prawns. The wine list should satisfy anyone's taste.

Diners are constantly reminded of the age of the hotel by the array of relics that could have been dredged from great-grandfather's attic. Old photos and paintings depict the Washoe House of yesterday, and ancient signs, posters, stuffed animals and off-beat memorabilia are lingering mementoes from an era of the old west.

Roadside inns such as Washoe House sprang up like mushrooms during California's early years, but the completion of the transcontinental railroad in 1869 eliminated the need for them. Washoe House is one of the few that has survived.

Washoe House, Stony Point Road and Roblar Road, Petaluma 94952. (707) 795-4544. Eight miles north of Petaluma on Highway 101 take the Gravenstein Highway exit (Highway 116); drive 1.5 miles west to Stony Point Road, then 2 miles south to Roblar Road. Restaurant only. Lunch served every day 11 A.M.–2 P.M.; dinner 6 P.M.–10 P.M. Monday through Saturday, 4 P.M.–10 P.M. Sunday. Bar.

UNION HOTEL

OCCIDENTAL

When I feel like gorging myself on good Italian food, I skip breakfast and lunch and head for Occidental. This sleepy little town in the backcountry of Sonoma County really comes alive at dinnertime. Three family-style restaurants compete for the hordes of visitors that converge on the village each weekend to tackle the mountainous seven-course dinners.

The historic restaurant of the trio is the Union Hotel. The box-like frame building was built in 1876 as a grocery store; it was later used as a dance hall and then as a boarding house. The town was a bee-hive of activity in those days, with lumberjacks busily harvesting the tall redwoods and the "carbonieri" making charcoal to fuel the timber-laden trains to their destinations. These workers were mainly skilled Tuscan and Lombard immigrants from Italy. They roomed and ate at the Union Hotel, stuffing themselves on the home-cooked meals and jugs of fine wine.

When the redwoods were depleted, the immigrants stuck around to become farmers and ranchers and the town's leading citizens. Their lusty appetites were the inspiration for today's famous dinners. The Panizzera family started it all in 1925; they offered gigantic meals at the Union Hotel for bargain prices. The idea was so popular and the crowds so great that other establishments sprang up to handle the overflow.

The Union's standard entrees are posted on a sign at the front of the dining room. The choices are chicken, duck, steak, spaghetti, or ravioli dinner. Last time I went there I chose the duck. With it came French bread, a large tureen of soup, a bean and lettuce salad, hors d'oeuvres and a plate of ravioli. In addition to the duck was a side order of stewed chicken, a plate of vegetables, some potatoes, and zucchini-fritters. For dessert, the sugar-dusted banana fritters were irresistable.

Just getting to Occidental is a memorable experience. The town lies in a forested canyon approached through pleasantly wooded pastures, farmland, and vineyards. Several country roads, which are made almost tunnel-like by the overhanging trees, lead to the little town and its endless feasts.

Union Hotel, Main Street, Occidental 95465. (707) 874-3662. From U.S. 101 and Santa Rosa, 7 miles west on Highway 12 to Sebastopol, 6 miles west on the Bodega Highway to Freestone, then 3.5 miles north on the Bohemian Highway. Restaurant only. Dining room open 11:30 A.M. –9 P.M. every day.

The
Bay Area

TO MENDOCINO

TO EUREKA

TO SACRAMENTO

Inverness

**INVERNESS
LODGE**

Crockett

*Port
Costa*

**BURLINGTON
HOTEL**

CASA MADRONA
SAUSALITO HOTEL *Sausalito*

Oakland

San Francisco

**PLEASANTON
HOTEL**

Pleasanton

BED AND BREAKFAST INN
JACKSON COURT
THE MANSION HOTEL
RED VICTORIAN
SPRECKELS MANSION
UNION STREET INN
WASHINGTON SQUARE INN

San Jose

LA HACIENDA *Los Gatos*
INN

TO SANTA CRUZ

THE BAY AREA

It's no wonder that the San Francisco Bay Area is the locale more frequently chosen for vacations than any other part of the state. Every aspect of its environment bombards the senses with pleasurable stimuli. The landscape of hills and water, toyed with by golden sunsets and creeping fogs, is a magnet for adventurers. The region is not completely taken over by urbanization, and there are excellent stretches of unspoiled territory only minutes from the big cities.

For those who are not enraptured with high-rise hotels but who want to stay in touch with the city, there are two country inns in Sausalito. From there, visitors have quick access to both worlds—the many attractions and cultural activities of San Francisco and the pastoral qualities of the Marin County countryside. The great outdoors is all around—along the shores of the Golden Gate National Recreational Area, on Angel Island, among the towering redwoods at Muir Woods, and atop Mount Tamalpais, from which low-lying fogs can be seen spreading like blankets over the bay.

The western edge of Marin County is dominated by the Point Reyes National Seashore, sometimes called "the greatest meeting between land and sea." It's a world of its own, a realm of marshlands and tidepools, rolling moors, sandstone cliffs, dense summer fogs dripping from pines and firs, and the ever-present thunder of the surf. The weather is cool, and the average temperatures vary only four degrees from summer to winter. The little community of Inverness is the gateway to the seashore, and fortunately has a country lodge of its own.

On the opposite side of the Bay, a ridge of regional parks separates the East Bay cities from the hilly terrain beyond. Mount Diablo, the highest point in the Bay Area, rises out of this terrain, and its picnic grounds and tip-top observation point are accessible by car. Surrounding the base of the mountain are quiet, peaceful back roads bordered by old cemeteries, farmhouses, wooden fences, groves of buckeye trees, grazing cattle and the sites of old ghost towns, all within touring distance of the revived ghost town of Port Costa.

South of San Francisco, Skyline Drive follows the ridge of the Santa Cruz Mountains. There the traveler has breathtaking views down into the sprawling South Bay cities on one side and the serene coastal foothills on the other.

The climate does its part in making the Bay Area a year-round playground. Temperatures rarely fall outside of the range of forty to eighty degrees. Only the rainy season, from November to April, causes some concern, but rainy days are perfect for visiting such history-filled places as the Oakland Museum. It has the most intriguing collection of exhibits on California art, history, and nature to be found in the state—a full day's worth of entertainment.

INVERNESS LODGE

INVERNESS

One of the most beautiful drives in Marin County is the wooded country lane that follows the shore of Tomales Bay out onto the windswept Point Reyes peninsula. The only town between the junction with the Coast Highway (Highway 1) and the tip of the peninsula is the scenic little village of Inverness, which has been a popular resort community since the turn of the century, when summer homes dotted the hillsides and several big shingle-style lodges and hotels catered to the vacationers who were unable to buy their own pieces of the pie. The town has retained its resort qualities, and Bay Area residents pour into the area during the summer on their way to the beaches.

The last of the shingle-style lodges is the secluded Inverness Lodge. It was built shortly after 1900, and was once a favorite resort and hunters' hangout. The lodge nestles in a grove of laurel, oak and acacia trees on a hillside overlooking Tomales Bay. A steep narrow street winds its way up to the rustic old lodge and its intimate little restaurant, called Manka's, which makes the place all the more European in feeling. Milan and Manka Prokupek started the restaurant many years ago, and the tradition is carried on by their son, Milan, Jr., and his wife Judy.

The Czechoslovakian and Viennese-style dishes served at Mankas are masterpieces of gourmet cooking, and they are complemented by the unhurried, relaxed atmosphere of the restaurant. Even during the winter, the rainy, stormy moods of the weather add their own appeal and make the roaring blaze in the fireplace a welcome treat. Dinners include hors d'oeuvres selected from a buffet table loaded with cheeses, fruit, marinated herring, salads, relishes and breads. The hot soup of the day is served with warm rolls. Entrees are prepared with the generous use of wines and spices. Along with the local delicacy, Tomales Bay oysters, and roast duckling or leg of pork, veal is a prominent dish. It is cooked either in mushrooms and wine or in a paprika sauce. As a finale, the dessert cart is wheeled around for a selection from the assortment of Czech pastries.

An equally inspiring treat after sunrise is in store for overnight guests. The unique breakfast menu includes such exotic early-morning delights as crepes filled with raspberry preserves, dumplings with onions and eggs, and fresh fruit accompanied by bacon and sautéed mushrooms on toast with a split of champagne.

The lodge has four guest rooms on the upper floor furnished with pieces as rustic as the inn itself. A couple of these open onto a sundeck where a glimpse of the bay is visible over the treetops. Out back are several woodsy guest cottages tucked under the trees.

The pinewoods character of the area around Inverness is everything that it used to be. The early-century summer homes, with their lingering charm, are still identified by names like Edgemont, The Gables and Quail Point. The hilly roads couldn't be more pleasant for walking or riding bicycles, particularly in the spring, when foxgloves and forget-me-nots show off their annual color on the hillsides. It's all a perfect setting for the old country lodge.

Inverness Lodge, Callender Way and Argyle Streets, Inverness 94937. (415) 669-1034. From the Bay Area take the Stinson Beach exit from U.S. 101 north of Sausalito, then follow Highway 1 through Mill Valley along the coast to Olema. Turn left on Bear Valley Road; drive 6 miles to Inverness. Lodging on the European plan; inexpensive to moderate. Four lodge rooms with private baths; 5 cottage units. Breakfast and dinner served to the public (dinner reservations required). Restaurant closed Tuesday and Wednesday; open only on weekends during the winter. Close to Point Reyes National Seashore, Morgan Horse Farm, hiking, biking, fishing, sailing, clamming. Inverness Music Festival is held in the summer.

SAUSALITO HOTEL

SAUSALITO

Since the turn of the century the Sausalito Hotel has occupied its watch-dog site just off the main street in the busy little bayside town. In the early days, Sausalito, watched over by impressive hillside mansions, was still mostly open countryside, but the waterfront was a bustling transportation center where steam trains to and from the north country exchanged passengers with the San Francisco ferryboats. Tourists pouring into town to wait for the autoferries caused traffic jams that were not to be believed. The main strip was a flourishing, bawdy corridor of bordellos, saloons and gambling dens catering to transients, dockworkers and incoming sailors. During Prohibition, bootleggers such as "Baby Face" Nelson rumbled past the hotel with truckloads of contraband headed for the ferry dock and a midnight run to the City.

And the Sausalito Hotel was in the middle of it all. No doubt the guests who, over the decades, have peered from the corner bay window could collectively write the history of the town. Who knows what part the hotel itself played in these colorful activities?

Today, some things remain the same. The stately old mansions, or what's left of them, still keep watch on the town; tourists continue to flood into the intriguing community; and the weekend traffic jams haven't gotten much better. A multitude of fine shops, galleries, restaurants, pubs, and crafts shows attract people in droves from the big city to the little one.

Guests at the hotel couldn't get any closer to the action, nor could they find a more rewarding base for exploring the Riviera-like village. The hotel's unobtrusive entrance in the Mission Revival façade leads up a steep, narrow staircase to the second floor lobby of the waterfront inn. The hotel doesn't provide meals, only rooms, and every one is delightful. Most impressive is the corner, streetside room furnished with the huge elaborately carved bedroom set that once belonged to General Grant. The ensemble is a relic from Grant's days on the west coast, and has ended up in the hotel's superb collection of fine Victorian antiques. All the other rooms have personalities of their own, some with bay windows that look into the park across the street, others with a view of the bay.

A little legwork or bicycling will soon uncover the offbeat qualities of Sausalito. The search could begin anywhere—around the floating colony of houseboats, which range from elegant to derelict; in the secluded dining and drinking patios behind the mainstreet façades; on the overhanging decks of the hillside restaurants; or in the small community park where the assortment of characters around the elephant statue makes Sausalito people-watching hard to beat.

Sausalito Hotel, 16 El Portal, Sausalito 94965. (415) 332-4155. Lodging includes continental breakfast and free parking; moderate to expensive. Ten rooms with private baths; 5 rooms share 3 baths in the hall. Each room has a wash basin. Close to quaint shops, ocean beaches, Golden Gate National Recreation Area, Muir Woods, Mt. Tamalpais, sailing on the bay. Directly across the bay from San Francisco.

CASA MADRONA

SAUSALITO

Not all of Sausalito's charm is prominently displayed on busy Bridgeway Avenue. To find some of the more delightful secluded spots, you have to retreat through the passages between buildings and up the steep, narrow steps, or following the twisting streets that zig-zag their way around the hillsides. One of the inconspicuous hideaways hidden among the trees is the Casa Madrona, a grand old mansion from Sausalito's past. It sits precariously on the side of the hill above town, commanding a sweeping view of San

Francisco Bay.

A lumber baron named William Barrett built the handsome Victorian building in 1885. Not much is known about Barrett's life, but most likely the house was an expression of his readiness to retire and settle in the town. The result is an elegant, richly detailed mansion showing off his accumulated wealth and stature. Barrett gave the house its name. In those days, all the fancy homes of the upper class had names. Deliveries from the market were dispatched, not to numbered addresses, but to Sea Point, Holly Oaks, or Casa Madrona.

J. P. Gallagher converted the residence into a hotel in 1911. Rather than creating a finely appointed hostelry, Gallagher was satisfied with a nondescript, anonymous sort of place. Quite possibly it operated as a bordello, much like those that were flourishing along the main strip early in the century.

The present owner of the hotel restored the building to its former elegance and created a country inn with a reputation for a very French atmosphere. The hillside setting, the outdoor decks, the rooms without baths, all add to the European charm. But the most tasteful touch is the renowned French restaurant, called Le Vivoir, that occupies the bottom floor. The delicious aromas wafting upwards from the restaurant are quite tantalizing, and the exceptional entrees have made Le Vivoir one of the most respected dining spots in the Bay Area for good French cooking. The atmosphere is very romantic, and the outdoor terrace, with its bright yellow umbrellas, is a pleasant place to have drinks.

Some of the lofty hotel rooms have an overwhelming view of the bay; others face into the treetops. They are furnished rather simply with dainty provincial pieces worthy of the French decor. From the glassed-in parlor, you can look down on the busy

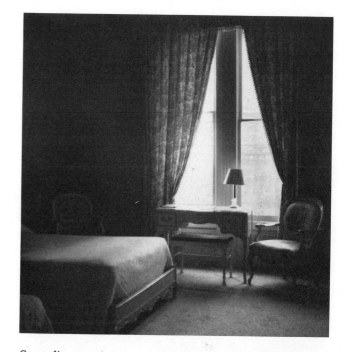

Sausalito tourist scene and the colorful array of boats in the marina. The Casa's airy perch gives guests a feeling of privacy and solitude. Visitors shouldn't be surprised if they bump into a noted celebrity or two taking advantage of the seclusion.

Casa Madrona, 156 Bulkley Ave., Sausalito 94965. (415) 332-0502. Lodging on the European plan; moderate. Several rooms have private baths. Dinner served to the public at Le Vivoir, daily 6 P.M. –10 P.M. For dinner reservations call 332-1850 (reservations advised). Close to quaint shops of every kind, Golden Gate National Recreation Area, Muir Woods, Mt. Tamalpais, sailing on the bay. Directly across the bay from San Francisco.

THE INNS OF SAN FRANCISCO

San Francisco is fortunate to have a number of small bed-and-breakfast inns. They are comparable to European family-run "pensions," with as much home-like character and charm as their foreign counterparts. Travelers making the rounds of California's inns will find that these urban hostelries provide an extension of their country-style enjoyment while they are visiting "the city by the bay." As in European pensions, not every room will have a private bath. Most inns serve a continental breakfast, and each gives personal attention to the special needs of travelers.

The Bed and Breakfast Inn was the first of the small San Francisco inns. Its six rooms are located in two quaint old houses that sit side by side and date back to pre-earthquake days. The inn is located on a quiet cul-de-sac just a few doors off Union Street, one of the most interesting shopping streets in the city.

4 Charlton Court, San Francisco 94123. (415) 921-9784. Moderate to expensive.

Jackson Court, formerly the Callahan Mansion, is entered through a courtyard. Eight beautiful rooms have names such as the Safari Room, the Blue Room and the Library. Reservations require a minimum stay of one week.

2198 Jackson Street, San Francisco 94115. (415) 931-6406. Moderate.

The most unusual inn is **The Mansion Hotel** (*above*) in Pacific Heights. This fancy three-story Victorian has sixteen rooms named after local historical characters. It is often frequented by celebrities, from movie stars to politicians. Events here have included book parties, magic shows and concerts, with the proprietor himself playing the musical saw. In the front yard are several intriguing sculptures by the late Beniamino Bufano, San Francisco's own colorful, beloved and often controversial sculptor. A small museum displaying his art is adjacent to the hotel.

2220 Sacramento Street, San Francisco 94115. (415) 929-9444. Moderate to expensive.

The Red Victorian is the only San Francisco inn within walking distance of Golden Gate Park and its many attractions. The 1904 hotel is in the heart of the Haight-Ashbury district, where "flower children" frolicked over a decade ago. The area is undergoing a renaissance and now has many unusual shops, boutiques and restaurants.

1665 Haight Street, San Francisco 94117. (415) 864-1978. Moderate to expensive.

Five elegant rooms have an Edwardian charm at the **Union Street Inn**. A continental breakfast is quite relaxing in the sunny garden setting behind the inn, which is located in the midst of the fine restaurants, fascinating shops and hilly neighborhoods of old San Francisco.

2229 Union Street, San Francisco 94123. (415) 346-0424. Expensive.

On the east side of Washington Square sits the **Washington Square Inn** in the colorful North Beach section. It is near the cable car line that runs between Fisherman's Wharf and downtown. Of the fifteen guest rooms, several have bay windows that provide views of the park and neighboring hills.

1660 Stockton Street, San Francisco 94133. (415) 981-4220. Expensive.

The Spreckels Mansion (*above*) is a grand old Victorian built in 1887 for the Spreckels family (of sugar fame). All five guest rooms have extraordinary views. Some rooms have fireplaces, sitting areas, chandeliers, stained glass windows and potted palms. Wine and hors d'oeuvres are served in the library in the afternoon.

737 Buena Vista West, San Francisco 94117. (415) 626-5460. Expensive.

BURLINGTON HOTEL

PORT COSTA

It hardly seems possible that the sleepy little town of Port Costa was once a grain capital and bustling seaport. In the 1880s and '90s, three thousand laborers loaded California's wheat and barley crop onto the largest ferryboats in the world. The ferries were headed down the Carquinez Strait to the San Francisco Bay, and from there to all parts of the globe.

Late in the nineteenth century, George McNear made the town what it was, laying out the streets, building wharves and warehouses, and introducing the shipping industry. Out of his efforts grew the lusty, hell-raising port community, with its rowdy, boisterous dockworkers providing the action. Over the years, however, several devastating fires crippled Port Costa, muting the original atmosphere. The fifth and last one, in 1941, burned for a week, and the town never recovered from its effects.

One of the few original buildings near the waterfront is the Burlington Hotel. It was lucky; it survived the five big holocausts. No one seems to know just how the Burlington got its name. The railroad tracks are only a few yards away, and although railroads did own hotels in the area, neither the Burlington Railroad nor any other line ever had a known connection with the hotel. But the hotel did provide transient lodging to the railroad and dock workers, and as late as 1926 the restaurant was feeding five hundred stevedores each day.

Construction of the hotel was started in 1876 and wasn't finished until four years later. The architect applied his knowledge of eastern Victorian design, but wasn't very keen on structural details. The bay windows, for example, almost fell off in the 1960s, because they weren't tied into the structure properly; the problem has since been corrected.

The Burlington certainly didn't miss out on the town's notorious and bawdy past. Brawls were commonplace in the hotel bar, where dockworkers, sailors, and railroad men battled among themselves. Big-shot entrepreneurs did their wheeling and dealing here in smoke-filled rooms as they tried desperately to corner the wheat market. Madame Fayette once brought her "girls" over from Oakland along with a sea captain who gave a rousing party at the hotel. The party ended three days later and the captain skipped out, leaving Madame Fayette holding a bill for several hundred dollars. It took her and her troupe a week to raise the money, using their own resourceful means, but the tab was paid.

Bill Rich, the present owner, has revived Port Costa and its hotel and made them what they are today. The ex-truck driver and genius of foresight bought the old warehouse, the sandstone bar, and the Burlington in the 1960s when activity in the town had dwindled to almost nothing. He restored all the buildings and rented parts of the warehouse for use as antique shops and restaurants. The village is now a beehive of activity, particularly on weekends.

The Burlington Hotel satisfies the needs of those who want to stick around for a day or two. After picking up a key at the bar inside the warehouse, the visitor climbs the steep stairs to the second- and third-floor guest rooms. A nice glow fills the hallways from the large stained-glass skylight over the stairwell. All nineteen rooms are filled with the unusual collector's items that Bill Rich has accumulated over the years.

When George McNear reigned over the town, not one of his hotels had a Room 13 because McNear had a superstitious fear of the number. But Bill Rich has solved that dilemma, a traditional one for hoteliers, by naming all the rooms after women. "Kaye" has a big wrought iron and chrome-plated bedframe, and a sunny sitting area that opens into another bedroom for use as a suite. "Margaret" has a shady look to it, with the red decor and the round bed hiding behind a curtain of beads. All the rooms are decorated with vintage photos and prints, homey old antiques that have been around for several lifetimes, and a lot of unusual clutter, some of which you may have trouble identifying.

Port Costa is not much more than a main street stretching three or four blocks from the highway to the waterfront: "town" would be something of a misnomer—it's more like a tree-lined residential lane with a few charming old businesses near the water's edge. The pace is slow. Once you've made the rounds of the antique shops, there is not much to do except drink at the bar or lounge on the benches in front of the hotel and watch the curious parade of tourists come and go. Bicycles seem like the most appropriate form of transportation, and the crooked hilly roads are quite obliging for working up an appetite.

The little community gets more popular every year, so you won't be alone driving the scenic, twisting back road along the bluffs above Carquinez Strait.

Burlington Hotel, 2 Canyon Lake Drive, Port Costa 94569. (415) 787-9973. Three miles east of Crockett and Interstate 80. Lodging only; inexpensive to moderate. Five rooms with private baths; 14 rooms without. Numerous antique shops and two restaurants in town. Close to John Muir House (6 miles), Briones Regional Park (9 miles), Benicia antique shops (11 miles).

PLEASANTON HOTEL

PLEASANTON

After all these years of growth and change, Pleasanton is still a "pleasant town," with its tree-lined Main Street and blend of historic old buildings and inviting new shops. In the early part of the century, the "all-American" appearance of this country town attracted hordes of filmmakers and movie stars to the area, creating a major industry for the rural community. Mary Pickford, Charlie Chaplin, Abbott and Costello, Tom Mix and Buster Keaton were a few of the big names who arrived for the production of such memorable old movies as *Rebecca of Sunnybrook Farm*.

Only one of the old hotels that fed and sheltered the late-show heroes and film crews still exists. It sits under the big trees beside Dry Creek. The establishment used to be called the Farmers Hotel, and was rebuilt soon after the original burned in 1898. One of the colorful owners was Paul "Bouquet" Cohn, a gambling boss and underworld figure whose stature attracted professional gamblers to the private parties he held in the upstairs rooms.

After a more recent fire, the interior was redone and the name was changed to the Pleasanton Hotel. You can't spend the night there anymore, but you can enjoy the atmosphere of its restaurant, the finest in town. Old and new touches have given the sophisticated dining rooms an elegant feeling. The walls are covered with huge antique mirrors and local art. Green plants and fancy chandelier lamps hang from the rich wood ceilings. The narrow old-style windows have been replaced with large picture windows that look into the lush garden surrounded by magnolia, kumquat and strawberry trees. The garden has become a popular setting for wedding ceremonies. Receptions are held afterwards in the hotel's ballroom.

The food is excellent and plentiful, and there is something for everyone: steaks, sautéed dishes and one of the largest selections of seafood outside of Fisherman's Wharf.

The traditional weekend brunch-buffet is a particular treat. Here you can help yourself again and again to the assortment of fresh fruits, salads and many meat dishes, such as beef stroganoff, barbequed chicken, corned-beef hash and even ham and eggs.

The restaurant is entered through the weathered wooden doors, past the dark and cozy saloon. The giant mirror in the white, pillared back bar reflects a lot of good times for the long-time clientele who crowd in each weekend to enjoy live musical entertainment.

Pleasanton Hotel, 855 Main Street, Pleasanton 94566. (415) 846-8106. Restaurant only. Lunch, Monday through Friday, 11 A.M.–3 P.M.; dinner, Monday through Thursday, 4 P.M.–10 P.M.; Friday and Saturday, 4 P.M.–11 P.M.; Sunday, 2 P.M.–9 P.M. Sunday brunch, 10 A.M.–2 P.M. Reservations suggested.

LA HACIENDA INN

LOS GATOS

The Saratoga-Los Gatos Road is a nicely wooded drive that has always been the main route between the two towns. At the turn of the century, stagecoaches followed its path alongside that of the Interurban Railroad that connected the peninsula communities. Both modes of transportation brought many guests to the inn at the foot of the Santa Cruz Mountains.

The inn was built as a semi-Japanese style complex in 1901 by Theodore Morris. He called it Nippon Mura Inn, meaning "Japanese village." He worked as an agent for a Japanese company and spent a great deal of time in the Orient. His fondness for the architectural style and detailing he saw there inspired him to construct the lodge and its village-like grouping of cottages and stables on thirty-two acres of forested grounds. It became a popular stagecoach stop for Bay Area tourists who were starting out on the long climb over the mountains to the coast.

A subsequent owner gave the Nippon Mura Inn its new name, La Hacienda, in 1941. The place is now a blend of cultures—Oriental building details, Mexican name, and a continental dinner menu.

The crowds that flock to La Hacienda Inn these days are indicative of the pleasurable feast that is served. But there's room for everyone. The restaurant is spread throughout the old lodge and is capable of seating 250 people at a time. The dining area is divided up, making possible an intimate evening of conversation and good food.

The menu includes complete dinners as well as a la carte items. Some of the specialties are veal scaloppine with fresh mushrooms, sweetbreads cooked in wine, roast duckling, chicken sauté, coq au vin and broiled salmon. Full dinner selections include soup, salad, relish plate, spaghetti, entree with vegetables, and dessert.

The original bungalows are long gone, but lodging is available next door to the restaurant. Although the cottages were recently built and are contemporary in character, they do blend with the old lodge and provide a chance for guests to linger a day or two, enjoying the numerous sights in the area.

"Old Town," in Los Gatos, is a restored mission-style school that houses a multitude of unusual shops, craft studios, outdoor displays and an amphitheater. A few miles west of the inn are the Villa Montalvo Arboretum, the antique shops of Saratoga and the Paul Masson Winery and tasting room. Even the giant redwoods at Big Basin Redwoods State Park, twenty-four miles west, are not out of reach.

La Hacienda Inn, 18840 Saratoga-Los Gatos Road, Los Gatos 95030. (408) 354-9230. Two miles west of Los Gatos. Lodging on the European plan includes continental breakfast; moderate. All rooms have private baths. Contemporary motel with TV, swimming pool, private patios Historic restaurant serves lunch, 11 A.M.–3 P.M.; dinner, 3 P.M.–11 P.M.; Sunday brunch, 11 A.M.–2:30 P.M. (Dinner reservations recommended; [408] 354-6669.) Hakone Japanese Gardens nearby, Mission Santa Clara (11 miles), old mercury mining town of New Almaden (15 miles).

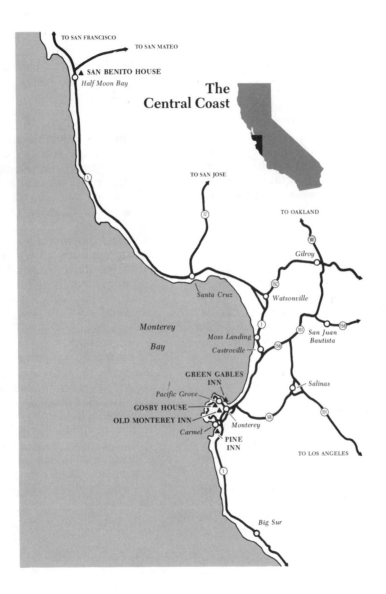

TO SAN FRANCISCO

TO SAN MATEO

▲ **SAN BENITO HOUSE**
Half Moon Bay

The
Central Coast

TO SAN JOSE

TO OAKLAND

Gilroy

Santa Cruz

Watsonville

Monterey

Bay

Moss Landing

*San Juan
Bautista*

Castroville

**GREEN GABLES
INN**

Pacific Grove

GOSBY HOUSE

Salinas

OLD MONTEREY INN

Monterey

Carmel

**PINE
INN**

TO LOS ANGELES

Big Sur

THE CENTRAL COAST

The fascinating California coastline prompts many tourists to choose the coastal route as they travel south from San Francisco towards Monterey Bay. The stretch between Half Moon Bay and Santa Cruz does not have quite the awesome ruggedness of the cliffs along the Big Sur area. However, the route does hug the ocean's edge and pass by fields of brilliantly colored flowers, pumpkin patches, tiny secluded beaches and the winter habitat of elephant seals at Año Nuevo State Reserve.

There is much to see and do on the north side of Monterey Bay. At Santa Cruz there is the mission, wharf, playland-at-the-beach, and a main-street garden mall filled with beautiful shops. North of Santa Cruz, the dense woods contain picnic sites at Henry Cowell Redwoods State Park and the authentic Roaring Camp steam train at Felton. Art galleries, attractive shops and a gentle surf draw crowds to the seaside resort town of Capitola. Several beaches south of Aptos are gems of the California coast, with warm waters and safe swimming areas.

Highway 1 parallels the arc of Monterey Bay between Santa Cruz and Carmel. It passes through a fertile vegetable-growing region where roadside stands display enticing bargains for a variety of produce. By itself the little hamlet of Moss Landing makes a picturesque fishing village scene, but it is unfortunately overshadowed by the giant smoke-stacks of an ill-placed power plant.

Sand dunes mark the northern approach to the history-filled Monterey Peninsula, where three resort communities attract thousands of visitors to their pine-woods environment.

Carmel is the center of attraction. The unique character of the town comes from the hundreds of tiny shops tucked away in courtyards and narrow corridors, the intimate little restaurants, Hansel and Gretel architecture, and the proliferation of galleries that offer the best in art, photography, and hand-made crafts done by local artisans. A visit to Carmel will require advance planning. The quaint inns are very popular, and summer weekends are booked weeks ahead. Holidays are impossible there unless you really plan early.

Most of the peninsula's history is rooted in Monterey, in the old Spanish adobes and in the Cannery Row made famous by John Steinbeck. This abandoned complex of fish canneries has been transformed into a series of interesting shops and bustling restaurants incorporating the theme of the bay.

Pacific Grove is noted for the annual migration of monarch butterflies that arrive there in October to spend the winter in the big pine trees. The town has many nineteenth-century mansions, shingle-style buildings and a stone lighthouse built in 1855.

Seventeen Mile Drive is the scenic parkway link between these seaside communities. The winding toll road loops around the peninsula and along the unspoiled shoreline of sandy beaches and rocky outcroppings. For trips outside of the area, the spectacular Big Sur coastline and Hearst Castle at San Simeon are worthy of a day's outing.

The weather adds a dramatic touch of its own to the central coast landscape. The fog helps temper the summer heat and mingles photogenically with the cypress and pine forests. Temperatures seldom reach the uncomfortable point and remain rather moderate year round but visitors are advised to carry a coat or sweater.

SAN BENITO HOUSE

HALF MOON BAY

The coastal town of Half Moon Bay is world famous for its pumpkin patches. Fields of orange color appear during October, when the fall season is climaxed with the annual Pumpkin Festival. Thousands of Bay Area residents pour into the community for a weekend of parades, pie-eating contests, craft fairs and a last chance to pick a Halloween pumpkin.

During the rest of the year, the town's charm is enough to entice visitors in search of antiques, local crafts, good restaurants or fun on nearby beaches. Until recently, Half Moon Bay was without any semblance of country inn accommodations for properly putting up tourists. That need was filled, however, when the old Mosconi Hotel was restored as the San Benito House.

The hotel dates from the 1870s and was one of the first lodging houses in the small community. Estanislaus Zabella constructed the hostelry after laying out the town. He was an influential and enterprising gentleman who married into the family that held the original land grant. The original adobe village was called San Benito, but the name was changed to Half Moon Bay in 1872.

Today, Carol Regan is proprietor of the historic Mosconi Hotel. She and her partners in the venture chose to name it San Benito House in recognition of its early heritage. The hotel provides more than just excellent accommodations. The saloon has been restored to replicate the original interiors shown in the old photographs that hang on the walls. Next door, picnic lunches can be ordered at the Garden Deli Cafe for excursions into the countryside. But the *pièce de résistance* is the splendid restaurant where lunch, dinner and Sunday breakfast are served to both guests and the public. The room is filled with butcherblock tables covered with blue paisley tablecloths. There are festive displays of breads, wines, nuts and cheeses sitting about. Tall French doors at the end of the room open onto a pleasant outdoor garden where lunch is sometimes served. Only two or three entrees are offered each evening for dinner, but they are prepared with the utmost attention and from the freshest produce and seafood available at the time.

Overnight guests arriving at the hotel's entrance on Main Street will find a telephone for making contact with the management. Check-in is handled in the kitchen, where the folksy, homelike atmosphere of the hotel becomes evident amid the aromas of country-style cooking. The guest rooms on the sec-ond floor reflect the mode of the past: travelers can recline on antique brass beds or soak in the large old-fashioned bathtubs. Additional amenities include a sauna and a glassed-in sun deck for sitting and reading, relaxing or watching the ocean in the distance.

There are many things to see and do in the area. The innkeepers will gladly make suggestions and provide information about side-trips. With the hotel in full operation, visitors can now be assured of a rewarding base for explorations.

San Benito House, Main Street at Mill, Half Moon Bay 94019. (415) 726-3425. Thirty-five miles south of San Francisco on Highway 1. Lodging includes breakfast; moderate. Eight rooms, six with private baths; one large suite with kitchenette. Historic walks, biking, boat harbors and piers, whale watching and clamming in season, backroads, Filoli gardens.

GOSBY HOUSE INN

PACIFIC GROVE

Pacific Grove has always struck me as being the quieter and more secluded community on the Monterey Peninsula. It stretches around the cypress-covered hills and along a spectacular section of the shoreline on Monterey Bay. The town got its start in the 1870s as a religious retreat. It was just a tent city then, striving to become as popular as Lake Chautauqua, the great Methodist training camp in New York. The western Chautauqua conferences were held near the center of Pacific Grove and in the old Chautauqua Hall which is still standing.

The finest accommodations in town are at the newly restored Gosby House Inn. It was built in the 1880s by J. F. Gosby, a shoe cobbler by trade, who worked out of his small shop a few doors up the street. He enlarged his home over the years and converted it to the town's first boarding house, serving the annual summer influx of Methodist ministers who came to the conferences.

The conferences played out by 1926 and the hotel lost its ministerial clientele. The community's charm, however, continues to attract tourists who come to gaze at the butterfly migrations, amble through the old lighthouse and travel the scenic Seventeen Mile Drive. Just strolling around the neighborhoods of old Victorian homes is a pleasant treat. Gosby House is a perfect home base for exploring the entire peninsula.

The seventeen rooms range from large to small, and all have the epitome of country inn furnishings. The Gosby Suite on the first floor is the fanciest in the house and has its own fireplace and tall windows overlooking Lighthouse Avenue. A couple of rooms on the second floor have views of the bay over the treetops.

Gosby House still has much of the feeling of a large Victorian home. A comfortable downstairs parlor looks as inviting as it must have in Mr. Gosby's day. Here, in the old armoire, you will find a beautiful antique doll collection, a proud possession of the owners. Photographs on the wall show the hotel during various stages of its existence. The parlor also serves as the setting for a continental breakfast each morning.

Inn-goers who appreciate the ambience of historic buildings will enjoy the restaurant next door to the hotel. Maison Bergerac, a Queen Anne-style home, was formerly the Hart mansion, but has been transformed into one of the most notable French restaurants in the country. Reservations must be made well in advance due to its popularity and limited seating.

Gosby House Inn, 643 Lighthouse, Pacific Grove 93950. (408) 375-1287. Lodging includes continental breakfast for guests only; moderate to expensive. Seventeen rooms, eleven with private baths; all rooms have wash basins. No smoking inside. Lovers Point Beach, Cannery Row, Point Pinos lighthouse, golf, tennis. Restaurants within walking distance.

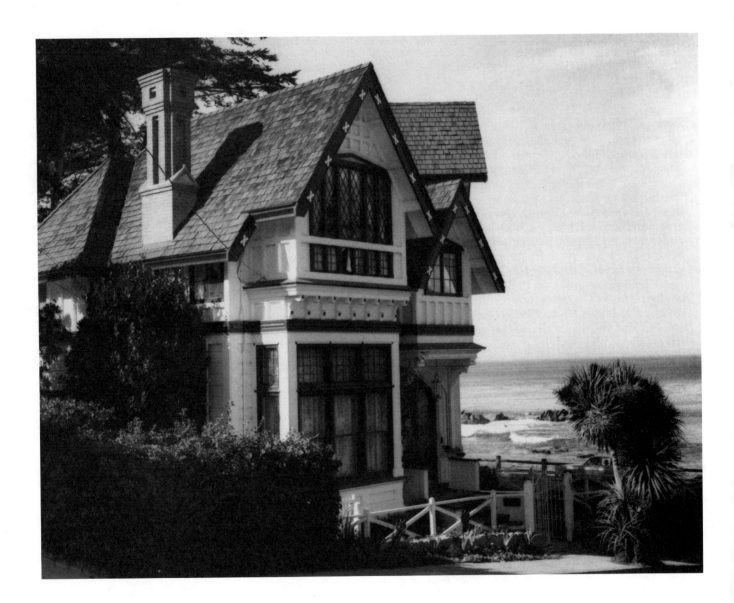

GREEN GABLES INN

PACIFIC GROVE

During the summer months visitors can enjoy the beauty and comfort of one of the fine old mansions that Pacific Grove is famous for. This half-timber, step-gabled Queen Anne-style residence has been around since the early resort days of the town, when huge hotels like the Del Monte and El Carmelo attracted tourists by the trainload.

Old records reveal that the house had many owners. William Lacey, of a prominent Monterey family, built the mansion, complete with chapel, in 1888. A Judge Wilbur from Pasadena used it as a summer home in the 1890s, when it was called Ivy Terrace Hall, a reference to the expanse of ivy that cascaded down the hill toward the bay. Three Carr sisters lived there after Wilbur; they were allegedly an eccentric trio. Then the Gerrard family took over, making many of the improvements that have kept the mansion sturdy and sound and up to date. The estate became an inn for the first time in 1958 when John Flatley rented out several rooms on weekends. Many movie stars and public figures stayed there from time to time.

Mr. and Mrs. Roger Post live in the house now and quite generously turn three of its rooms into guest accommodations each summer. Each room—the Balcony Room, Garrett Room and Gable Room—is furnished with splendid antiques and served by a bath in the hall. The view of Monterey Bay from the house is a superb display of the coastal shoreline, and the lapping waves are only a few yards away.

This little inn is a far cry from the big lavish Del Monte that once thrilled vacationers. But with its intimate charm it makes a rewarding base for those who come to enjoy the piney woods, sandy beaches, barking seals, challenging golf courses and the recreational potential of the area, which haven't changed much since the early part of the century.

No meals are served at the inn, but guests will find two very nice restaurants set in other old mansions in Pacific Grove. The Maison Bergerac on Lighthouse Avenue, near the center of town, offers gourmet French cooking. Consuelo's, also on Lighthouse near Cannery Row, combines Victorian splendor and Mexican cuisine.

Green Gables Inn, 104 Fifth Street, Pacific Grove 93950. (408) 375-2095. Open during summer only. Lodging only; moderate. Three rooms with community bath. Close to the Seventeen Mile Drive, Carmel shops, restaurants, Monterey's Cannery Row, historic adobes, ocean beaches, Point Lobos Reserve State Park. Feast of Lanterns is held in Pacific Grove in July.

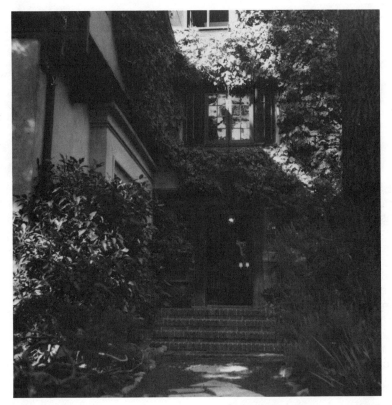

OLD MONTEREY INN

MONTEREY

On a quiet side street, away from the activity of downtown Monterey, a rambling Tudor mansion sits majestically under sprawling California oaks. This beautiful home was built in 1929 by Carmel Martin, a highly dedicated civic leader and mayor of the city from 1911 to 1913. His mother had always admired the country manor architecture of England, so he instructed his architect to design a house reflecting that style.

After his death, and several owners later, the house ended up in the possession of Gene and Ann Swett. Over the past ten years the Swetts have shown an affection for the home greater than that of any owner since the Martins. They have patched and repaired every square inch of the long-neglected structure. The grounds are once again lush thriving gardens of colorful foliage, manicured lawns and ivy-covered slopes cascading into the creek.

When their children grew up and moved away, the Swetts decided to make the house available to peninsula vacationers as the Old Monterey Inn, the town's only "country inn." The designation is fitting enough, considering the secluded nature of the house on spacious grounds shaded by dense trees and shrubbery. Hardly any of the surrounding residences are visible from the guest rooms and gardens. The inn is the only such facility that has met the city's strict requirements of what an urban inn should be.

There are many delights that make this inn an intriguing architectural showplace. First to catch your eye are the massive timbers, a foot square, used as posts and beams in the vestibule. Tall French doors and windows give the rooms a light and open feeling. In the dining room, the ceiling is made up of various designs stamped into stucco-like panels. Adding to the interior elegance are the fine craftsmanship and hand-carved designs on the stairs' newel posts. These were done by August Gay, a local artisan. He also carved and painted several window valances in an almost folk art manner.

The guest rooms are particularly interesting and comfortable. Each has a large bed covered by a goosedown comforter and a choice of pillows, firm or soft. Small sitting areas allow guests to relax in the seclusion of their rooms. Every room has a name influenced by its character. The Library has the greatest appeal to guests because of its fireplace, bookshelves, windows all around and its own small sun deck. The hallways are enriched with old engravings picked up at local auctions, and with superb Yosemite photographs taken by Mr. Swett's father. There are many little touches that inn-goers will recognize as having been inspired by some of the best of California's inns.

Recently, the children's much-used pool table was moved out of the attic space and into the downstairs living room, giving guests an equal chance to show their skill. The attic was then transformed into two charming hideaways with skylights, fireplaces, wicker furnishings and woodwork that was skillfully refinished to match the color and texture of that in the rest of the house.

Although privacy is a basic element of the inn, the dining room serves as a communal gathering spot. On pleasant mornings, the tables on the outside terrace where the warm sun filters through the trees, provide an even more appealing setting. The breakfast menu varies from day to day, but might include blueberry muffins, pastries, scones, fruit compote, brioche, or toast and ollalie berry jam. This berry is unique to the area, and the Swetts serve the jam as a special treat for visitors to the peninsula.

This is the kind of house that deserves to be experienced for its fine craftsmanship, richness of materials, and construction techniques that would be impossible to duplicate today. There is a lasting impression to be gained by living briefly in the country home atmosphere of this Monterey landmark.

Old Monterey Inn, 500 Martin Street, Monterey 93940. (408) 375-8284. Take the Munras exit from Highway 1, turn left on Soledad, then right on Pacific for approximately six blocks to Martin St. Lodging includes breakfast for guests only; expensive. Seven rooms, three with private baths. Historic adobes, Fisherman's Wharf, Cannery Row shops and restaurants, Seventeen Mile Drive. Captain Jacques and Gallatin's are two fine restaurants in historic buildings.

PINE INN

CARMEL

Pine Inn is Carmel's oldest hostelry. During the 1890s, one portion of the existing complex sat further up Ocean Avenue and was known as the Carmelo Hotel. At that time, Ocean Avenue was nothing more than a rugged dirt path slashed through the pine forest. Only a few occasional visitors bothered taking the daily stage over the "devil's staircase" from Monterey.

Around the turn of the century, a couple of enthusiastic developers struggled to turn Carmel's isolated, pine-woods setting into an artist's paradise beside the sea. One of their first tasks was to move the Carmelo Hotel four blocks down the hill toward the ocean, where it became the nucleus for the Pine Inn. The woodsy shingle-style inn had its own tent village for summer guests and a large livery stable, since horses were still the major mode of transportation.

The idea of secluded living in the inspirational backwoods retreat caught on, and a Bohemian atmosphere flourished. Poet George Sterling, novelist Mary Austin and photographer Arnold Genthe were among the first on the scene, later followed by architect Charles Greene, Sinclair Lewis and Robinson Jeffers. Jack London made many trips to the town to visit and carouse with Sterling and his friends. The Pine Inn undoubtedly did its part in attracting potential residents who, until then, were rather put off by the town's lack of suitable accommodations.

The character of Carmel has changed somewhat over the years, and the Pine Inn itself looks a lot different today. The shingle-style façade was replaced with a more pristine look. Various additions and appendages now cover the entire block, creating pleasant spaces among the rambling wings.

In spite of the inn's reconstructed Victorian decor, numerous impressive antiques are scattered about, such as the old cast-iron fireplace in the cocktail parlor and the huge grandfather clock standing in the second-floor lobby. Guests are warmly welcomed by fresh-cut flowers. Landscaped terraces lead to intriguing penthouse suites. The lodging rooms have fancy wallpaper, brass bed frames and marble-topped dressers that add to the inn's elegance.

This is a bustling inn on the busy main street. It is larger than most of Carmel's inns. Several dining rooms within its walls attract crowds of hungry diners. Most popular is the Gazebo Room, which faces the courtyard. The roof of the room slides back to reveal blue skies during the day and the stars at night.

The partially enclosed courtyard and narrow alleyway passages are typical features of Carmel's architecture and are usually stuffed with small boutiques and art galleries.

Pine Inn, Ocean and Monte Verde Streets, Carmel 93921. (408) 624-3851. Lodging on the European plan; moderate to expensive. All rooms have private baths. Two dining rooms serve all meals to the public throughout the day. TV, cocktail lounge, no pets. Close to Seventeen Mile Drive, Monterey's historic adobes, Carmel Mission, golf courses, five blocks to the beach. Bach Festival held in July.

The Gold Country

Alleghany

KENTON MINE
LODGE

North San Juan

NATIONAL
HOTEL

RED
CASTLE   Nevada City

HOLBROOKE   Grass Valley
HOTEL

TO RENO

Foresthill

WOODSIDE
MINE

Georgetown

GEORGETOWN
HOTEL

SIERRA
NEVADA   VINEYARD
HOUSE III   HOUSE

Coloma   TO LAKE TAHOE

Auburn

Folsom   Placerville

FOLSOM
HOTEL

Sacramento

ST. GEORGE
HOTEL

MINE HOUSE

Amador City   Sutter
Creek   Volcano

SUTTER CREEK
INN   NINE EUREKA STREET

Jackson

NATIONAL   Mokelumne Hill
HOTEL

LEGER
HOTEL   MURPHYS
HOTEL

Murphys   CITY
HOTEL

Angels Camp   Columbia
Sonora

SONORA
INN   GUNN
HOUSE

Coulterville

THE GOLD COUNTRY

Highway 49 links all those nice old Gold Rush towns that conjure up nostalgic visions of Bret Harte and Mark Twain tales. These colorful relics are about as close as anyone can get to experiencing California's past. Some are small sleepy villages such as Coulterville, Chinese Camp and North San Juan. They seem to be hardly more than ghost towns and scenic reminders of a long-gone era. Other towns, such as Auburn, Jackson and Sonora, are thriving places reflecting the spirit of mining days, though shiny aluminum store fronts are taking their toll.

Highway 49 itself changes from a freeway-type thoroughfare to the best of country lanes as it winds through the foothills of the Sierra Nevada Range. It traverses three hundred miles of historic countryside.

There are several key places in the Gold Country where tourists can get a feel for the role that mining played in the frenzied search for wealth. Most important is Coloma, site of the Gold Discovery State Park. This is where it all began, when a few specks of yellow metal were found in the tailrace of Sutter's Mill. The mill has been restored as a working replica, and many of the town's historic buildings have also been preserved.

Other significant mining sites shouldn't be missed. At Malakoff Diggings State Park, north of Nevada City, trails lead through the sculptured cliffs where hydraulic hoses were used to wash away the hillsides and expose the grains of gold. There are several acres of scenic ruins at the Empire Mine in Grass Valley, along with the magnificent stone and brick "Empire Cottage." The giant Kennedy Tailing Wheels near Jackson once lifted residue from the mine to a storage pond beyond the hills. And at Columbia State Park, gold panning is still a favorite pastime in this authentically restored mining town.

Summer days in the Gold Country are very hot, but evenings are pleasant. Springtime is the most enjoyable touring season. The rolling grassland is fresh and green then and wildflowers cover the hillsides. Crowds thin out in the fall, and the autumn foliage creates another colorful spectacle. Winter tends to be rainy and cold, but even the rains and fog create moods among the ruins that no photographer would want to miss.

KENTON MINE LODGE

ALLEGHANY

I drove the steep, dirt road out of Alleghany with my attention equally divided between the breathtaking descent into the canyon and the possibility of meeting another car on the narrow, twisting route. Foote Crossing Road really hugs the hillsides on the last stretch of the trip to Kenton Mine Lodge. As I approached the lodge on a brisk autumn morning, I realized I had arrived at a real gem of the Gold Country. Here in the pines along Kanaka Creek, the recently transformed buildings of a now defunct mine have become one of the most rewarding get-away places I know of.

History buffs will appreciate the lodge for its

primary attraction, the Kenton Mine, one of the oldest hard-rock mines in the northern Mother Lode. The site was settled by a group of Hawaiians back in 1850, which accounts for the name Kanaka Creek. Tunnelling started in 1860, and production continued off and on until 1939. The results of the last period of activity would have been worth over sixteen million dollars on today's gold market. From 1939 until 1970, the camp was used to house men working at the nearby Oriental Mine, the last mine in the state to shut down.

The lodge buildings consist of the nine-bedroom boarding house, where bachelor miners lived; seven cottages that housed families; the cook's quarters and dining room; and the superintendent's house. These original wood-frame buildings, dating from the early thirties, are in amazingly good condition, but restoration is an on-going project. Interior refurbishing reflects the simplicity of the miners' existence and was handled with exceptionally good taste through the use of an exciting antique collection scattered throughout the buildings. The rooms in the boarding house are cozily furnished with lace curtains, bright patchwork bedspreads on beautiful old bedframes, and some unusual items of furniture made by the miners themselves during their leisure hours. A couple of elegant brass beds were actually used by the company cook and his dog.

Guests are served family-style, home-cooked meals in the cookhouse at long tables where everyone can get to know each other. Films, guest speakers and informal seminars are occasional diversions in the Mine Tavern. Or, for a little variety, you can mosey up the mountain to Casey's, the local memorabilia-stuffed saloon in Alleghany. This venerable old town was the only one in California where gold mining was still the principal occupation after World War II.

The footbridge over Kanaka Creek leads uphill past the mine opening to the topside entrance of the stamp mill, the most interesting of the mine buildings. This spectacular structure, built of heavy timbers and cascading several stories down the hill, was erected in 1934 in only two month's time. Here ore from the mine was crushed and pulverized so that the precious gold could be extracted. Very few old stamp mills are accessible to the public, and touring this one is a special treat for guests of the lodge.

Gold pans get a real workout along the creek, and who can resist the expectations of finding glittering, yellow flakes among the grains of sand? But there are plenty of other activities, such as the stiff, challenging hike to the top of Lafayette Ridge, good for whetting the appetite. You can also explore abandoned mine and cabin sites, lazily fish for trout in the gurgling stream, or get married under the pines, as some couples do.

It's hard to break away from the peaceful seclusion of this historic canyon and the rustic old mining camp. Nature and history combine forces to create a perfect setting for an enjoyable outing in the mountains.

Kenton Mine Lodge, P.O. Box 942, Alleghany 95910. (916) 287-3212. Take Highway 49 north from Nevada City to the turnoff about five miles beyond the town of North San Juan, then turn right on the road to Alleghany. In Alleghany, take Foote Crossing Road—first road on the right as you enter town—for 2.5 miles to the lodge. Open all year. Lodging on the American plan includes all meals for guests; inexpensive. Nine boarding house rooms share 5 baths; 7 creek-side cabins. Activities are hiking, gold-panning, fishing, swimming, campfires, and special mine tours for guests. Non-guests are welcome to visit.

NATIONAL HOTEL

NEVADA CITY

From the freeway that sweeps into town, you can spot the golden, turnip-like dome at the rear of the National Hotel. The dome was a part of the annex that once sat beside the hotel facing Broad Street. The freeway wiped out the annex and the dome was moved to the rear.

The National was built in 1854 by Zeno Philosopher Davis, and it has the distinction of being the oldest, continuously operated hotel in the state. Zeno's brother Alexander was the contractor for the building, and fired the bricks in his kiln out near the Pittsburg Mine. In 1856, two years after construction, a big fire started in a storeroom full of cigars and burned everything except the brick shell of the hotel. The place was rebuilt, but in 1863 another fire did $25,000 worth of damage. The hotel was again restored and opened to the public. It continues to add its share of charm to an old mining town rich in history and Victorian buildings.

The hotel played a big role in the development of the town, acting as a nucleus for the wheelings and dealings of miners and merchants, and the general activity associated with a bustling Gold Rush community. In the early 1860s, headquarters for the stage line was located on the first floor. A gong in the lobby alerted passengers that it was time to board the coaches for such colorful diggings as Red Dog, Rough and Ready, Timbuctoo, Yankee Jims, and French Corral. These same stages brought the miners into town to gamble away their fortunes in the hotel. Old-timers recall seeing as much as $50,000 in gold coin and dust stacked up in the gambling room, where the dining room is now located. Eight million dollars in gold passed over the bar in one thirty-five year period.

In the early days, National Alley ran alongside the building leading to the stables where the stage teams were kept. It's rumored that other stables, housing fillies of a shadier reputation, also operated behind the hotel.

The National was local headquarters for the political campaigns of Lincoln in 1864 and Grant in 1868. Big ceremonies were held here, and many influential people attended. Bonfires lighted the streets, and rallying citizens marched up to the hotel from Grass Valley carrying flaming torches.

Such sights are a rarity now, but tourists never cease to be fascinated by the picturesque town and its old hotel. Perhaps because the National has had so few owners, its charm and early character has remained intact. Dick and Nan Ness, the current owners, are carrying on the tradition of preservation.

If you can't get a room at the hotel (and you probably can't without reservations), at least drop in and rest in the second-floor lobby, with its great pendulum clock and grand piano. Or have a drink in the downstairs bar under the coffered tin ceiling and watch the parade of local characters ramble in and out. The elegant back bar came from the Spreckels mansion in San Francisco. Next door is the dining room, one of several places in town for lunch or dinner.

Every room in the hotel is interesting. Some are small and cozy, others spacious with an adjacent sitting room. All represent the Victorian era truly, with their velvet and marble trappings, flowered wallpaper, red carpets, and canopied beds. Guests have a particularly good vantage point on the outside balcony for watching the Independence Day Parade and the Father's Day Bicycle Classic.

On my visit, I spent the day touring side-street antique shops, having lunch at the fascinating American Victorian Museum, and just wandering around the pleasant hilly streets before returning to the hotel for dinner. On weekends the town comes alive with various forms of nighttime entertainment. At several spots musicians offer combinations of country, folk and rock music. The National itself caters to the swing-dance crowd. In this town which was once the third largest in the state, Nevada City's dwindling population hasn't lost its ability to entertain us flat-landers.

National Hotel, 211 Broad Street, Nevada City 95959. (916) 265-4551. Lodging on the European plan; inexpensive to moderate. All rooms with private baths. Victorian Room serves lunch and dinner to the public. Saloon, TV, swimming pool. Antique and crafts shops, historic buildings. Independence Day Parade and Fathers' Day Bicycle Classic held in town. Empire Mine in Grass Valley nearby.

RED CASTLE

NEVADA CITY

Tourists gaze with fascination at the red brick house on Prospect Hill overlooking Nevada City. Nothing else in town compares architecturally with the gingerbread façade, steep sloping roofs, and white icicle trim dripping from the eaves. I climbed the zig-zag path leading up to the house from Deer Creek, hoping to learn the story of the Red Castle and its conversion into a small inn.

John and Abigail Williams built the luxurious house in 1860 as a prestigious residence for their prominent-lawyer son. For the pioneer family, completion of the house was the fulfillment of a twiceshattered dream. First their savings had been diverted to rebuild downtown properties destroyed in the big fire of 1856; then again in 1858, to repair their flooded gold mine. But their third effort at accumulating the necessary funds was a success, and the four-story house and its landscaped gardens became a reality.

I could tell by the hand-cranked doorbell that the mansion was a true relic of the Gold Rush era. And what a beauty it is! The Gothic Revival building looks as good today as it did during its years of glory. The former owners, Mr. and Mrs. James Schaar, purchased the house in 1963 and were responsible for most of the restoration work that has kept the house looking so well preserved.

Restoring the structure's former elegance was no easy task, since the house was in an advanced state of dilapidation. Efforts in refurbishing the verandas, fancy trim, and brickwork resulted in what the Smithsonian Institution calls a "perfect restoration." Places where bits and pieces that had been removed or replaced were identified, and pieces were installed to match the originals. Porch flooring was relaid precisely as before, and bricks were removed, cleaned, and after the deteriorating mortar was replaced, returned to their original positions.

This historic landmark doesn't look like a castle, but its stately position on the hill no doubt inspired the romantic name. Visitors are treated to a marvelous experience, not the least of which is the superb view of the town from the lofty site.

Jerry Ames and Chris Dickman recently became the new owners of the Red Castle. They set out to liven up the interiors by introducing, in keeping with the Victorian era, vivid colors and wallpapers to the stark white rooms. Along with many of the original antiques, Ames and Dickman have integrated furnishings of a more eclectic nature to replace some of the authentic period pieces that yielded little comfort. In addition, they have added two new guest rooms—the Garden Room and Gold Room—to the original five. Home-baked breads from the kitchen highlight the continental breakfast served each morning.

The Red Castle is the oldest surviving brick home in Nevada City. It still retains as much richness and grandeur as ever and evokes nostalgic visions of what the social life on the hill was like during its early days.

Red Castle, 109 Prospect Street, Nevada City 95959. (916) 265-5135. Lodging includes continental breakfast; moderate. Five rooms with private baths; 2 rooms share bath. Close to antique and craft shops, historic buildings and homes, American Victorian Museum, scenic hilly walks, live music in town.

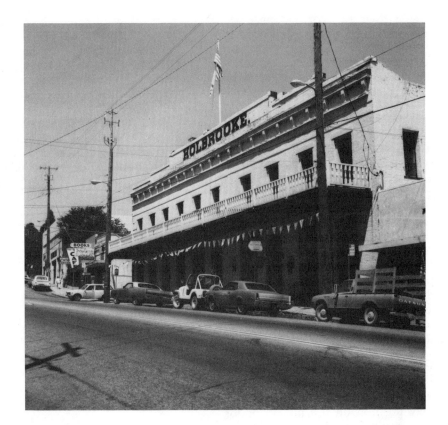

HOLBROOKE HOTEL

GRASS VALLEY

The Holbrooke today should definitely be seen. Except for the fact that it no longer rents rooms to travelers, the hotel stands as a reflection of the past and a tribute to the citizens who brought it to life again.

The Holbrooke dates from 1851. It was housed in two separate buildings then—the Golden Gate Saloon and the Adams Express Office. They were rebuilt as one after the big fire of 1854 destroyed them along with most of Grass Valley. By 1862 the building had become known as the Exchange Hotel; it had been given a new brick façade and attained its present form. Brick had come into vogue after the fire, and heavy iron shutters and sod roofs were added as extra precautions. Dan Holbrooke and his wife bought the hotel in 1879 and their name has been attached to it ever since.

The Holbrooke was a classy and elegant way-station for gold barons, wealthy travelers, Presidents, and gamblers, as well as those still in search of fame and fortune. The names of Mark Twain, Bret Harte, Ulysses S. Grant, James Garfield, and Black Bart are among the famous, and infamous, that show up in the old registers.

Over the years, time and unsympathetic owners ravaged the hotel's façade, but it has now been put back in order, restored as closely as possible to its original appearance. Mrs. Arletta Douglas, along with her preservation-minded friends, decided that the building had a lot of life left in it. They set about restoring the iron balcony across the front, replacing doors and windows as they once were, and refurbishing the saloon, with its copper walls and the ornate back bar that was shipped around the Horn from Italy. The sweeping, mahogany staircase was given a fresh look, and a delicate iron-cage lift was added. This full treatment revived the hotel to its former glory.

In the Holbrooke Dining Room visitors can feel the real elegance of the hotel as they pass through the wide arches into the dining area. The plush carpets, lace tablecloths, and high-backed chairs enhance the luxurious atmosphere. The beautiful richly colored walls of exposed brick were once covered by an accumulation of plaster and wallpaper put there by previous owners.

The Holbrooke is an experience in first-class dining, although the prices are not exorbitant. Special little touches have been added to make the meal distinctive, from the fresh-baked bread and homemade soup to the tangy ice cream dessert. A good selection is available, including steaks and seafood —lobster, stuffed sole, a variety of shrimp dishes— as well as Beef Bourguignon and sweetbreads. The wine list offers a healthy selection of California wines. The Holbrooke is one of the few places that serves Cherries Flambé for dessert—an elegant way to end a meal.

In the lobby is a display of mementos from the hotel's past. Of particular interest is the old register showing that Benjamin Harrison, Grover Cleveland, and boxers James Corbett and Robert Fitzsimmons signed in on the same day. It is believed that they were headed for a big sporting event further north. No doubt they all enjoyed dining at the colorful Holbrooke a century ago as much as visitors do today.

Holbrooke Hotel Dining Room, 212 West Main, Grass Valley 95945. (916) 272-1989. Restaurant only. Lunch Monday through Saturday, 11 A.M.–2 P.M.; dinner, Monday through Sunday, 5 P.M.–10 P.M. Sunday brunch, 11 A.M.–3 P.M.

FOLSOM HOTEL

FOLSOM

Sutter Street in Folsom had its days of prosperity in the 1860s and '70s, when the town was a busy financial and transportation center and the jumping-off point to the Mother Lode mining camps. The street, at the center of town, was the hub of activity—stores, banks, hotels, and saloons thrived on the trade created by the railroad terminus there and the gold strikes nearby. This is where the action was, and the town became the third largest in California.

When the Gold Rush ended, the town held its own, but spread out away from Sutter Street. By the 1960s the strip was almost a ghost-town scene, but some folks of vision realized that a bundle of charm was left in the frontier-style architecture. They converted the abandoned buildings into antique and gift shops, a soda parlor, restaurants, galleries, and the Gaslight Theater. This rousing theater revives the theatrical scene of an earlier era as melodramas, vaudeville and musical productions play to packed houses on Friday and Saturday nights throughout the year. The quaint old Southern Pacific Depot now serves as a visitors' center, helping strangers find their way around the historic street that has once again come to life.

There used to be competition from several hotels on Sutter Street, but the only one to survive was the Folsom Hotel. It was built in 1886 by Charles Zimmerman after its predecessor, the New Western Hotel, burned down that year. The hotel only cost Zimmerman $7000 to build and was advertised as "home of the working man and stranger." Today the old hotel has been freshened up and has several rooms, including a bridal suite, each with a big old-fashioned brass bed. The dining room features a Basque-style dinner every night, and the bar is just next door.

Folsom sits in a sea of rolling grassy hills in close proximity to the large Folsom Dam Recreation Area, a great attraction to boaters, fishermen, swimmers, and hikers. Downstream, salmon can be seen fighting their way up the fish ladder at Nimbus Fish Hatchery during the autumn months. Historic Sutter Street is blocked off on certain summer weekends, and the avenue becomes a busy bartering place for the annual Flea Market, Peddlers' Faire and Antique Show. Sacramento and its newly restored Old Town is only twenty miles away.

Folsom Hotel, 703 Sutter Street, Folsom 95630. (916) 985-2530. Twenty miles east of Sacramento via U.S. 50. Lodging on the European plan; inexpensive. All rooms have private baths. Restaurant serves lunch and dinner to the public. Saloon. Close to many antique and gift shops, depot museum, Gaslight Theater, Folsom Lake Recreation Area.

WOODSIDE MINE

GEORGETOWN

The Woodside Mine is slowly evolving into a country inn. The task of restoring and refurbishing an old historic building is not always an easy one. But, the innkeepers now have two of the eventual seven guest rooms ready for overnight lodging and are continuing with their plans to establish a fine hostelry in the tradition of English country inns.

The building's history as a hostelry goes back to the 1860s, when the first structure on the site was called the American Hotel. It was one of several impressive hotels in town and served as a stagestop for coaches traveling the Wentworth Springs route to Tahoe. The American waged a nip-and-tuck battle for survival during the big fire of 1897, one of many fires that plagued Georgetown during the 1800s. The large trees beside the hotel acted as a buffer and kept the fire from destroying the building. However, it did get peppered rather badly by nails, bricks, and all sorts of junk when an explosion in a nearby store rocked the town. A couple of years later, in 1899, a spark from the chimney set the roof on fire and the hotel was destroyed. In a matter of three months the building that exists today was constructed, and the hotel was back in business.

As the Woodside Mine, the hotel is presently undergoing a thorough restoration—a new roof and foundation have been constructed, and some fancy decoration, such as the lacy, spiderweb brackets on the porch columns, were added. The new name has its origin in the mine that was operated by the Woodside Mining Company in the center of town during the 1860s. When nuggets-for-the-finding became scarce, the activity of this deep mine helped Georgetown maintain a respectable size.

The hotel is a stately and peaceful-looking building sitting at the end of the town's business section. All rooms have a homey atmosphere enhanced by their classical old country furnishings. Included in the room rate and served on the terrace is a hearty breakfast so that guests can start the day right before heading into the backcountry.

Since the Woodside Mine has limited accommodations at present, please call ahead for inquiries and reservations. The plans as outlined by the owners sound exciting and refreshing, and undoubtedly changes will be made as the hotel settles into its role as a country inn.

Woodside Mine, P.O. Box 43, Georgetown 95634. (916) 333-4499. From Auburn and Interstate 80 take Highway 49 south for 6 miles to Cool; then drive 12 miles east on Highway 193. At the corner of Main and Orleans Streets. Lodging includes breakfast served to guests only; moderate. Two rooms, one with private bath. Historic buildings, back roads, boating, swimming, picnicking, and fishing at Lake Edson (17 miles). Founders Day Celebration held in August; Scotch Broom (blooming bushes) tours in May.

GEORGETOWN HOTEL

GEORGETOWN

"Get a Widder at the Georgetown Hotel" read the sign on the float in the Coloma Days Parade. The hotel always seems to be the liveliest place in town; autos nestle around the building like horses around a watering trough. The saloon is the real center of activity; here city dudes mix with loggers and lumberjacks and bluegrass or country music is the mellow entertainment.

The current Georgetown Hotel is the third on the site, and was immediately rebuilt after the fire of 1897. It faces the broad Main Street, which was widened in the town's early days to prevent fire from spreading across the roadway.

Georgetown used to be a flimsy "tent town" down in one of the lower canyons. It was known as Growlersburg then because gold nuggets seemed to growl in the miners' pans. The townsite was relocated to its present position on higher ground after the big fire of 1852, started by a photographer's flash powder as he attempted to photograph a dead man in one of the gambling dens. Respectability and permanence eventually came to the rowdy mining camp, and Georgetown grew into the "Pride of the Mountains," a community that outdid nearby Placerville with its cultural and social life.

The stageline across the mountains to Auburn made a regular stop at the hotel, and the saloon was no doubt just as popular then as it is now. The beautiful old back bar and beer cooler were stashed away in the basement during Prohibition, but have since been brought out of hiding and restored to their proper settings.

Overnight guests should prepare for a somewhat spartan experience, compatible with that of the Gold Rush era. The community bathrooms, for instance, with their giant-sized claw-foot bathtubs, are at the end of the hall. The rooms, however, are interesting and comfortable. Almost every one is furnished with a big antique bed of wood or brass with a brightly colored bedspread, a fancy bureau, standing mirror, and lace curtains that flutter in the breeze.

I spent a long active day traveling the back roads between Georgetown and Wentworth Springs. The first stop was Volcanoville, an old Gold Rush relic with a sizeable population of about two, and a tiny photogenic little cemetery. Then on through the forested countryside, past the early townsites of 12 Mile House and Uncle Toms, to Wentworth Springs and the ramshackle remains of the old stagecoach stop.

Back at the Georgetown Hotel, dinner is served in the back room, and before long the pool table is popping and someone has a guitar or fiddle in hand. The hotel is a real antique—every time some local rowdy rides a horse into the bar, you can't help but feel that things haven't changed a bit from the early days.

Georgetown Hotel, P.O. Box 187, Georgetown 95634. (916) 333-4373. From Auburn and Interstate 80, take Highway 49 south for 6 miles to the town of Cool, then drive 12 miles east on Highway 193. Lodging on the European plan; inexpensive. All rooms share community baths. Dining room serves lunch and dinner to the public. Dinner, 5:30 P.M.–9:30 P.M. except Thursday. Mining towns, forested back roads, historic buildings nearby. Founders Day Celebration held in August, Scotch Broom (blooming bushes) tours in May.

SIERRA NEVADA HOUSE III

COLOMA

Just a half-mile north of Coloma is the architectural descendent of one of the town's leading hotels during the Gold Rush days. The original Sierra Nevada Hotel was built in 1850 and stood in the center of Coloma.

Governors, judges, generals, and senators gave open-air political speeches from its long balcony to the audience below. Shortly after the hotel was built, it was purchased and operated by Robert Chalmers before he built the famed Vineyard House on the opposite side of town. The Sierra Nevada had its finest days under his ownership during the 1850s. Fancy cotillion balls with full orchestras were held in the spacious hall, and carriages were sent to fetch the ladies from nearby towns and ranches. Chalmers was a teetotaler and didn't allow a bar in the building, a rather unusual policy for a hotel owner of that era, considering the endless clientele of thirsty, hardworking miners. Chalmers' sons took over in 1865 and promptly corrected the situation.

A long line of different proprietors ran the hotel until it burned in 1902. It was rebuilt immediately on the same site, but fire leveled it again in 1926. The present hotel was constructed in 1963 and was built just outside of town, since its original site, along with all of Coloma, has been preserved as a state park. Despite the new location, Sierra Nevada House III was reconstructed to look as much like its earlier counterparts as could be determined from the few old photos that still exist.

Sierra Nevada House does a particularly lively and spirited business in the summer as a result of the old-fashioned soda parlor on the ground floor. Tourists, seeking refuge from the beaming sun, order phosphates and sassparillas, or such special ice cream concoctions as the Miner's Delight, Gold Strike sundae and Bonanza Split.

The hotel is encircled at the second floor by a wide veranda, a typical feature of frontier buildings. Opening onto the veranda are six guest rooms for overnight visitors. Each room has flowered wallpaper and nice old heirloom pieces, but there has been no sacrifice of modern conveniences.

The public dining room serves delicious meals with tossed salad, homemade biscuits, and miners' beans in a dimly lit atmosphere surrounded by sketches and relics of early Americana.

Besides offering good meals and lodging, Sierra Nevada House has a couple of interesting treasures of the Gold Rush era worthy of museum display. Most impressive is the gigantic gold scale in the dining room. This huge, four-foot-wide mechanism weighed much of the 13 million dollars in gold taken from the Pacific Mine near Placerville.

In the parlor adjacent to the dining room hangs an impressive 600-pound mirror, its elaborate frame embellished with baroque carvings. It just may be the legendary Gold Hill Mirror which supposedly perished in the fire that destroyed the Isabell Saloon.

During the big search for gold in the 1850s, hotels were numerous and thrived on the miners' good fortune. Today the tourists keep the survivors as active as ever. Phase III in the life of Sierra Nevada House seems to be going well, since the historic town of Coloma attracts plenty of history buffs to the tranquil valley.

Sierra Nevada House III, P.O. Box 268, Coloma 95613. (916) 622-5856. One mile north of Coloma on Highway 49 at Lotus Road. Lodging includes breakfast; inexpensive. Six rooms with private baths. Dining room is open to the public. Lunch, 11:30 A.M.–2:30 P.M.; dinner, 5 P.M.–9 P.M. Closed on Monday and Tuesday between Labor Day and April. Soda fountain, bar. Close to Gold Discovery State Historic Park, museum, historic buildings, picnic grounds. Gold Discovery Days held in January.

VINEYARD HOUSE

COLOMA

A superb winery once occupied the site on which the Vineyard House was constructed. It all started when Martin Allhoff arrived from France in search of instant wealth on the California frontier. Like a lot of other disenchanted miners during the Gold Rush, Allhoff gave up mining and decided to make his fortune in a more domestic way. He created a 160-acre vineyard, whose reputation quickly spread throughout California and Nevada. Some of Allhoff's wines were so excellent that they were exported to France. A few years later, Allhoff's business agent in Virginia City was indicted for alleged tax and license violations. When Allhoff went there to offer his help he found himself in the same predicament. The offense wasn't all that great, but the wine-grower's brooding over the impending shame and embarrassment to his family ended with his tragic suicide.

Robert Chalmers married Allhoff's widow and took over the property. He continued to operate the prize-winning winery, and it expanded into one of the largest in the state. In 1878 he built the Vineyard House to serve as his home as well as an elegant hotel. The twenty-five by ninety foot ballroom was the scene of many gala social events. When throngs of people came to Coloma for the unveiling ceremonies of the nearby Marshall Monument, hundreds took turns having lunch at tables in the main dining room while the Governor and other dignitaries made speeches.

Robert Chalmers became one of Coloma's leading citizens, a dedicated politician and a member of all the prominent fraternal organizations. Sadly, his last days were clouded by insanity, another tragic event in the saga of Vineyard House.

The Chalmers and Allhoffs are buried in family plots in the Coloma cemetery just across the road from the inn. The graveyard is an interesting place to wander through; the old headstones and grave-markers of the pioneers tell their own tales.

In the early days of Vineyard House, the reputations of hotels were made by the quality of the meals they served; somehow, the word always spread in spite of primitive communication systems. Vineyard House had its share of the fame then, and the same high-quality home-style cooking is still being offered now, enhanced by the delightful experience of dining in the historic old mansion. Four intimate dining rooms follow the original room layout of the house; two of these were formerly a sitting and a sewing room. On a hot day, a nice breeze flows in off the long veranda, which is covered with grapevines that were planted in the 1870s.

On my visit, I was lucky enough to get in on the last of the special for the night, Chicken Sauté, a half chicken sautéed in mushrooms, sherry and gravy, and served with a big tureen of soup, salad, fresh-baked bread, and side dishes of vegetables. I've also heard good things about the shrimp Newburg sautéed in butter and sherry, and the chicken and dumplings. I was tempted to try the vegetarian dish, not because I'm a vegetarian, but many people are, and very few restaurants cater to their tastes.

Vineyard House is again operating as a hotel for visitors converging on Coloma to see Sutter's Mill and the Gold Discovery State Park. Upstairs the living quarters have been coverted into seven guest rooms furnished with original antiques rummaged from the attic or donated by friends. Typical of an old-fashioned country hotel, the bath is at the end of the hall. A saloon is located within the cool brick walls of the basement. The hotel makes an enjoyable retreat for an outing to "where it all began."

Vineyard House, P.O. Box 176, Coloma 95613. (916) 622-2217. On Cold Spring Road near the junction with Highway 49 in Coloma. Lodging on the European plan; inexpensive to moderate. Seven rooms share a community bath. Dinner served to the public Wednesday–Thursday, 6 P.M.–9 P.M.; Friday–Saturday, 5 P.M.–11 P.M.; Sunday, 5 P.M.–9 P.M. Jailroom Bar open Wednesday–Sunday, 5 P.M. Near Gold Discovery State Historic Park, picnic grounds, historic buildings, museum. Gold Discovery Days are held in January.

MINE HOUSE

AMADOR CITY

The Mine House hasn't always served travelers. Early in the century it was the headquarters and office building for the superintendents of the Keystone Consolidated Mining Company. In this impressive building, on a hill overlooking Amador City, the company conducted the various business involved in processing gold from the mine.

After the frantic scramble for nuggets of '48 and '49 subsided, Amador City got a brief rest until four off-duty ministers renewed the excitement all over again. The clergymen preached their Sunday sermons in the saloons and churches of the surrounding communities, then spent the rest of the week picking and digging in the banks of the gulches around town. It was the Baptist minister in the quartet who made the big find—he discovered gold embedded in chunks of quartz. This was an especially significant event since it led to the beginning of hard-rock mining in California.

Out of this "Ministers' Claim" grew the Keystone Mine, a consolidation of several mines in the area. It lagged at the beginning under various owners, but in 1866 the bonanza paid off. The extraction process produced $40,000 the first month and continued strong into the late 1880s, eventually producing a total of twenty-four million dollars' worth of the yellow metal. In 1942 the federal government closed the Keystone down along with all other mines to divert workers into the war. Ever since, the rusting headframes of the mine have stood idle on the hillside across the highway as a lingering reminder of the old days.

In 1955 the Peter Daubenspecks, from Michigan, were driving through the gold country on their vacation when they spotted the old abandoned brick building in a rather sad state of disrepair. Their ability to recognize its underlying potential was everyone's good fortune. They purchased the building and spent the next two years recycling the derelict structure into a country inn.

There are eight guest rooms in the building, and each one is unique, since its space formerly played a part in the processing of the gold. In the ceiling of the Mill Grinding Room, shaft supports are still visible from the days when the ore was pulverized here. The Vault Room contains the old walk-in safe where gold was stored to wait for the Wells Fargo stage to San Francisco. Gold was smelted in the Retort Room and lifted by dumbwaiter to the vault above; the keystone arch supporting the vault is exposed in the bathroom. Other rooms were used for bookkeeping activities and for assaying the gold. One served as a meeting room for the mine's directors, and another was a storeroom which has beautiful red brick walls. The Keystone Room was added after the turn of the century as temporary quarters for the mine superintendent's daughter and has pew-shaped headboards on the almost-matching twin beds. Every room has its own bath, private entrance, and fascinating items of antique furniture including ornamental chamber pots. When you punch a buzzer in the morning, a steaming pot of coffee is left outside the door.

The Daubenspecks are proud that oldtimers who worked for the Keystone Mine had read about the building's new use in newspaper accounts and returned to spend the night in the same rooms they once worked in.

Amador City is one of the smaller and more tranquil towns along this stretch of Highway 49. Aside from several antique shops, crafts shops, and a wine tasting room, most of the activity, including night life, is found in nearby Sutter Creek and Jackson.

Mine House, P.O. Box 226, Amador City 95601. (209) 267-5900. On Highway 49, south side of town. Lodging only; inexpensive to moderate. Coffee brought to guest-room door in the mornings. Eight rooms with private baths. Swimming pool; no pets. Antique shops, Gold Rush towns, autumn foliage, back roads nearby. Amador County Fair held in Plymouth during August.

SUTTER CREEK INN

SUTTER CREEK

Sutter Creek is one of those nice old Gold Rush towns that has somehow managed to escape the invasion of modern-day plasticity. The colorful, well-groomed buildings keep Main Street looking like a frontier scene of a hundred years ago.

In the midst of this avenue of antique shops, restaurants, overhanging balconies, and saloons from the swinging-door era, sits a little piece of the country—the Sutter Creek Inn. The charming house, surrounded by a spacious green lawn and a neatly trimmed hedge, has all the character you would expect from a true country inn.

The owner is Jane Way, a legend among patrons of these all-too-few, small-town hideaways. She created the inn from a New England style residence built of redwood in 1859 by the Keyes family. A prominent occupant of the house was Senator Edward Voorheis, who married the Keyes' daughter in 1880. One of his unforgivable deeds was the addition of a room to the left side of the house that somewhat spoiled the classic symmetry of the Greek Revival building. It is said that his wife was so upset she never set foot in that part of the house.

But, symmetry or not, the beautiful façade is only a foretaste of the refreshing experience that lies beyond. Entering the big inviting parlor is like walking into grandmother's house. Like most of the guest rooms, its decor is made up of interesting old furniture—not necessarily irreplaceable heirlooms, but just comfortable country-style furnishings. Some pieces were improvised from old objects put to unexpected and ingenious uses.

Behind the house is a grape arbor, shady lawn and several patios with benches. The two-story building at the rear was once the washhouse, and contains many of the guest rooms. They have such names as Upper and Lower Washhouse, Cellar room, Woodshed, and Miner's Cabin. Some of the rooms have cozy fireplaces and beamed ceilings, as well as Jane Way's famous "hanging beds," suspended on chains attached to the ceiling. These beds represent only one of the extra little touches that make the Sutter Creek Inn unique.

At 9 o'clock sharp, everyone gathers for breakfast around the long tables in the family-style dining room. On pleasant days the feast is held outdoors under the grape arbor, and the meal is a superb way to start the day. Breakfast is the only meal served at the inn, so guests have a chance to step out and explore other gastronomic possibilities along Highway 49. For lunch and dinner, a number of fine restaurants exist between Amador City and Jackson.

Sutter Creek is a friendly little town, and an ideal place to explore on foot, especially in the early morning hours and at dusk as an after-dinner treat. For a deeper investigation, pick up a copy of *A Stroller's Guide to Sutter Creek* at Mr. Tyler's card shop on Main Street. It points out a lot of details and features that you might miss otherwise. And like the Sutter Creek Inn, everything here should be enjoyed to its fullest.

Sutter Creek Inn, 75 Main Street, Sutter Creek 95685. (209) 267-5606. Lodging includes breakfast served to guests only; moderate to expensive. Thirteen rooms with private baths, four rooms without. No cigars, pets, or children under ten. Antique shops, restaurants, Gold Rush towns, back roads, lakes (20 miles), Daffodil Hill (13 miles).

NINE EUREKA STREET

SUTTER CREEK

Sutter Creek's residential areas are a stroller's paradise. Charm emanates from the classic old mansions that have a tinge of New England character, as well as from the impressive California-style bungalows

dating from 1918. The oldest homes lie within a block or two on either side of Main Street.

Eureka Street is only two blocks long, starting at Main and ending at the historic Knight Foundry. Along the way is a nice old house that accommodates many of the tourists who choose to linger in this frontier town. The house was built in 1916 by Tobias Lagomarsino of an Italian-American family that operated a stage route between Sutter Creek, Jackson and Volcano. He also opened the first steam laundry in town.

The inn, simply called Nine Eureka Street, is run by Helen Messick, no newcomer to innkeeping. Her inn is reminiscent of New England guest houses, where extra rooms in a private residence are rented to travelers.

Of the five rooms, the fanciest and most popular was formerly an open sleeping porch that was closed in with shutters and shades. The room is painted white, is very light and cheerful and has a big carved wooden bed. Another room in the dormer has beautiful twin iron beds and the windows overlook the front yard.

The living and dining rooms flow into one gracious area dignified by the original wood paneling and wood ceiling beams. The breakfront behind the long dining table has leaded panels of stained glass whose pattern is echoed by the front on the bookcases at the far end of the living room. The house has had few owners and few changes during its decades on Eureka Street.

Just a half block from the inn are the metal buildings of the Knight Foundry. It's been a Sutter Creek landmark since 1873. The machine shop is run by means of a water-powered Knight's wheel, the only operation of its kind in the nation. The workers recycle salvaged metal into iron castings for such uses as restoration parts at Old Town Sacramento and the state capitol building.

Nine Eureka Street, Sutter Creek 95685. (209) 267-0342. Lodging includes continental breakfast; inexpensive. Three rooms with private bath, two rooms share bath. Historic Gold Rush towns, antique shops, back roads.

NATIONAL HOTEL

JACKSON

The freshwater spring that bubbled from the ground where the National Hotel now stands was a welcome sight to nomadic adventurers and freight-wagon drivers in the old days. During their overnight drinking sprees, so many discarded bottles accumulated around the site that the settlement which eventually took root there was called "Botilleas." This name was considered somewhat undignified, and the town was later renamed Jackson, in honor of Colonel Alden Jackson, one of its early settlers.

The National Hotel, claiming an 1862 founding date, is still about the largest building in town. It sits imposingly at the end of Main Street. It was formerly known as the Louisiana House and was the scene of many colorful events. For example, when an alleged thief stole a horse from Evans and Askey, the hotel's proprietors, he was tracked down and captured near Nevada City. The posse brought him back, gave him a prompt trial on the porch of the hotel, and found him guilty. As with most horse thieves, he was marched to the nearby "hanging tree" and hung by the neck. The fact that he protested the verdict and produced a bill of sale made little difference to his executioners.

Mr. Askey was said to have been an incurable practical joker. At his urging, many an unsuspecting guest spent futile hours fishing for salmon in the creek behind the hotel.

The hotel's proximity to that creek was, at times, a cause for concern. Winter rains would saturate the ground such that any excess showers would cause the creek to rise and surge through the town. One such swell in the 1880s carried the National's outhouse and two dozen other buildings several miles down the canyon.

Jackson had the reputation of being a wild and woolly town well into the 1950s, when bordellos were doing a land-office business, slot machines were everywhere, and gambling was an open and active pastime. But, eventually things became much quieter —that is, until John Wayne and Glenn Ford came to town. After serving as grand marshals in one of Jackson's big parades, they became embroiled in an all-night poker game in the National's bar. When the smoke cleared in the early hours of the morning, the Duke had lost $26,000 to the local Ford dealer. Both cowboys retreated to the second floor and retired for the night in the "bridal suite," which fortunately has two large beds.

The National's forty-four guest rooms are comfortable and inexpensive, and they look about the way they always have. They serve as repositories for an extensive collection of ancient furniture and memorabilia gathered by Neil Stark, the hotel's owner and the town's number one antique collector. The pride and joy of the saloon is the big adjustable chandelier hanging over the bar. It came from Ohio and still burns kerosene.

While the springs were the center of activity in the old days, the bar dispensing liquids of a different sort is the center of Jackson's nightlife now. It's a rousing and lively place on Saturday nights, when the Gold Country tourists and the local regulars crowd in to whoop it up.

The restaurant in the basement still retains the name Louisiana House and serves good food in folksy surroundings. A large painting on the wall shows the National as it looked long ago when it had more of the character that went with the frontier townscape. In the 1930s the hotel fell victim to someone's remodeling whims. The red brick façade was plastered over and now bears little resemblance to the original.

National Hotel, 2 Water Street, Jackson 95642. (209) 223-0500. Lodging on the European plan; inexpensive. Thirty-six rooms with private baths, 8 rooms without. Louisiana House Restaurant serves dinner to the public; the hotel bar is also open to the public. Antique shops, Amador County Museum, Kennedy Tailing Wheels, Indian Grinding Rocks State Park nearby.

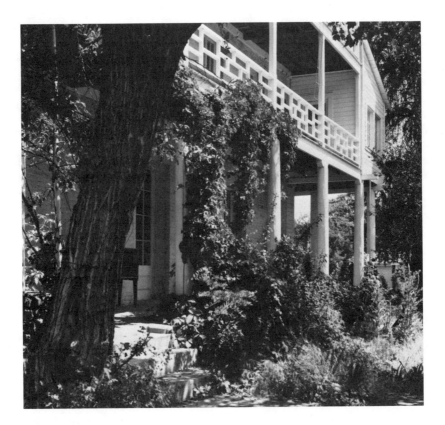

ST. GEORGE HOTEL

VOLCANO

Three times, hotels have risen from the ashes on the site of the St. George. It all started with the Eureka Hotel when, in 1853, this newly built two-story structure burned to the ground. There was no bell for alerting the citizens, and the firing of revolvers that was substituted sounded like nothing more than firecrackers. The fire spread so quickly that guests didn't even have a chance to remove their belongings, and the hotel was wiped out at a loss of five or six thousand dollars.

The replacement was also called the Eureka, but the devastating fire of 1859 destroyed this hotel too, along with other frame buildings that were parched from the lack of autumn rains. Volcano had a hook and ladder company by then. The firefighters' attempt to pull down adjacent structures to keep the fire from spreading failed, since they weren't able to haul the burning ruins out of the way in time.

Again the hotel was rebuilt, this time as the Empire Hotel. But this structure burned also. B. F. George tried once more in 1862. His creation, the St. George, is the hostelry that stands today, a hotel that refused to die.

Volcano has dwindled to a mere remnant of the town that once boasted a population of five thousand. Of its seventeen hotels, only the St. George is left. It's the town's most picturesque building; Virginia creepers and trumpet vines cling to the round porch columns and white veranda railings of the Monterey-style architecture. The vines turn a brilliant red in the fall.

Home-cooked dinners featuring prime rib and chicken are served in the folksy dining room, and the old parlor has a huge fireplace, supposedly built of seven dozen kinds of rock. The various-sized guest rooms on the second and third floors with their traditional frontier furnishings are rather unpretentious. The hotel is popular with groups getting together for Gold-Country outings.

About the only excitement in this colorful little mining town comes from the old-fashioned soda parlor that serves cooling refreshments on hot afternoons, a few small shops for souvenir collectors and a community theater. The activity is low-keyed and a refreshing change from the more spirited pace of busier towns. Volcano may seem to be just a notch above ghost-town status, but its sleepy character makes it all the more unique. Tourists love to travel the narrow, wooded back roads or spend an afternoon strolling along the main street and gazing at the silent stone ruins and time-worn buildings of the Gold Rush era.

St. George Hotel, P.O. Box 275, Volcano 95689. (209) 296-4458. Nine miles east of Jackson on Highway 88 to Pine Grove, then three miles north. Hotel and restaurant closed Monday and Tuesday. Lodging on the American plan; moderate. All rooms share community baths. (Several rooms in the annex have private baths.) Breakfast and dinner served to the public by reservation. A few shops in town, historical sites, autumn foliage, Indian Grinding Rocks (2 miles), and Daffodil Hill (3 miles).

LEGER HOTEL

MOKELUMNE HILL

Claim-jumping was such a widespread practice in this rich, gold-bearing area that none of the miners dared to leave their plots unattended. When they began to get rather hungry, one enterprising miner decided to make his fortune by hauling provisions. He bought a wagonload of goods and a tent in Stockton and returned to set up a trading post. Other businesses followed suit, and the Hotel Leger itself grew out of one of these early tent structures. It gained a more permanent form when a one-story stone building was constructed after the fire of 1854.

Mok Hill was a bad man's town, and murders

were frequent there. Fights over mining claims grew into full-scale conflicts, and only a vigilante committee existed to keep a lid on things. California's legendary bandit Joaquin Murietta used to show up in disguise in the Leger's saloon, and in others around town, and offer his opinions as to how the bandit Murietta could best be captured.

The Leger (pronounced Lay-zhay) has had more than its share of names. During the early days it was known as the Hotel de France, Hotel de Europa and the Union Hotel. It was called the Grand Hotel in 1874 after fire damaged it and destroyed the great hall at the rear. When it was restored in 1879, the present name was attached in honor of George W. Leger, the hotel's proprietor for twenty-eight years. Leger was responsible for purchasing the abandoned courthouse and expanding the hotel into it after the Calaveras County seat was moved to San Andreas in 1866.

The large hall that used to be behind the hotel was the scene of many lavish parties, balls and social events. Every year at Christmas time, a giant decorated tree stood in the hall, and a live Santa came down the huge chimney and handed out gifts to the spellbound children.

The Leger's lobby had the first electric lights in Mokelumne Hill. Most of the townspeople turned out to watch the illumination ceremony as lights stretched across the front of the building were turned on for the first time—quite an event in those days.

The hotel was completely restored and given a fresh look in 1960, though its authentic frontier character was kept intact. The restoration effort earned the Leger the Governor's Design Award for Rehabilitation, and a well-deserved award it was indeed.

Behind the colorful yellow façade with its white picket railings is a restful Victorian interior—a richly decorated saloon, guest rooms with an old-fashioned decor, and a scattered assortment of museum-like treasures. Some rooms have pleasant sitting areas with fireplaces and private baths. Others share baths, but all the rooms have the luxury of wood, marble and velvet trim. The good food and candlelit atmosphere of the dining room makes the hotel the most nostalgic place to eat between Jackson and Sonora. At the rear of the hotel a secluded swimming pool sits among the fruit trees and rock walls. Guests really appreciate its existence on hot summer days.

Sue Clark is the proprietor. Her goal is to expand the Saturday night performances in the Garden Courthouse Theater, next door to the hotel. A tradition of the hotel has been the presentation of plays by local theater groups attracting citizens from miles around.

Other equally historic buildings in the little town house a few interesting shops and galleries. For history buffs, the peaceful countryside and mining towns are accessible via back roads in all directions.

Leger Hotel, Mokelumne Hill 95245. (209) 286-1401. Thirty-eight miles north of Sonora on Highway 49. Take the historic route through town. Lodging on the European plan; inexpensive to moderate. Thirteen rooms, seven with private baths. Dining room open to the public for all meals. Swimming pool, saloon. Shops and galleries in town. Close to Gold Rush towns, Pardee and New Hogan Reservoirs.

MURPHYS HOTEL

MURPHYS

This old establishment was called the Sperry and Perry Hotel when it opened in 1856. James Sperry, of the Sperry Flour family, and John Perry built the stylish public house to accommodate curious travelers on their way to the newly discovered Calaveras Grove of Big Trees. Immediately after the grand opening, newspapers praised the owners for their commodious and elegantly furnished hotel, which served touring parties in such exquisite style.

At that time the town of Murphys was just recovering from the great Gold Rush; $20 million in gold had been taken from surrounding mines. Folks were beginning to turn to the more stable and domestic trades of farming, ranching and catering to the tourists headed for the giant sequoias and nearby caves. The hotel naturally became a success.

Only three years later, though, in 1859, an unfortunate setback occurred when a devastating fire destroyed the business section of Murphys along with most of the new hotel. The building supposedly had been fireproofed—iron shutters had been installed as a precaution against spreading flames. Townspeople had counted on the stone portion of the structure for protection, and had carried their valuables there for safekeeping. But the thick stone walls and metal doors were useless against the raging heat, and the hotel was gutted. When the fire broke through, everything was lost.

By 1861 the hotel was again serving the tourist trade. On request, the saloon keeper will gladly drag out the old registers containing some very distinguished names. C. E. Bolton, for instance, stopped over on February 8, 1880. That was about four years before detectives caught up with him for his acts as the gentleman bandit Black Bart. Ulysses S. Grant also visited the hotel in 1880, a couple of years after leaving the presidency. His appearance caused quite a commotion as half the town turned out to get a glimpse of the famous general. Mark Twain and Horatio Alger, Jr., spent the night here, as did John Jacob Astor, Henry Ward Beecher and Thomas Lipton, of teabag fame.

The hotel has seen activity equal to the best in western movies. Stages rumbled up Main Street to the front door bringing passengers, gamblers, and would-be miners from the lowlands. Gunplay occurred from time to time as local rowdies and badmen let off steam in the bar. The balcony across the front of the hotel was fancied as the best spot in town for watching parades and traveling medicine shows.

The hotel has, in fact, acted as an authentic western setting for the make-believe world of Hollywood on several occasions. Will Rogers filmed *County Chairman* here in 1932. That movie co-starred a freckle-faced kid named Mickey Rooney. Tom Tryon's movie *The Other* was shot on location in the area, and the crew of *The Day of the Animals* used the rickety old saloon and streets as a backdrop.

For a long time the place was known as the Mitchler Hotel. In 1963 it was sold to the Murphys Ale and Quail Club—a group of thirty-five college chums dedicated to preserving the historic landmark and perpetuating its hospitality.

The Murphys Hotel is an honest antique. It hasn't been overly modernized, and seems to retain more of its old-time character than most historic hostelries I've seen. Everything there looks ancient and undisturbed, yet the hotel is clean and comfortable. The rooms are filled with antiques that must be as old as the hotel itself, and the bathrooms are still down the hall. The Presidential Suite accommodated General Grant during his 1880 visit, and boasts a beautiful rosewood piano.

Weeknights are best for getting a good night's sleep at the hotel. The downstairs saloon does a rousing business on weekends, and the noise can be heard in the guest rooms well beyond midnight.

The lack of private baths, TVs, and telephones may seem like a comedown compared with the early years when the hotel was noted for its luxuries. In those days fresh vegetables were supplied by local ranchers and soft water was conveyed from a nearby spring. Sperry and Perry kept a snow-house at the Big Trees, and ice—the biggest luxury of all—was brought down to the hotel. But the Murphys Hotel of today wouldn't be half the experience if it totally conceded to the twentieth century.

Murphys Hotel, Murphys 95247. (209) 728-3454. Nine miles east of Highway 49 and Angels Camp on Highway 4. Lodging on the European plan; moderate. All rooms share community baths. Other motel units with private baths available. Dining room serves all meals to the public. Dinner, 5 P.M.–9 P.M. Old-fashioned saloon, historic buildings, museum in town. River running and fishing in the Stanislaus River, antique shops, Mercer Cave (1 mile), Moaning Cave (6 miles), Calaveras Big Trees State Park (15 miles), Columbia (14 miles), winter skiing at Bear West (Bear Valley).

CITY HOTEL

COLUMBIA

George Morgan built his two-story, red-brick building on Main Street in 1856 during Columbia's heyday as a mining community. The surrounding area had been ravaged in the search for gold, and buildings right in the middle of town were demolished by miners eager to get at the rich soil. George Morgan himself had a gold mine, but closed it when he discovered that his workers were secretly pocketing the gold and getting richer than he was.

The year after its construction, Morgan's building became known as the What Cheer House when P. G. Ferguson opened a liquor store in the lower floor. Through the years that space has housed a variety of businesses: the *Columbia Gazette*, an assay office, Cheap John Louis's Auction House, and Shine and Company's stageline office. The large hall on the upper floor nicely accommodated the Columbia Opera House. Not until 1871 was the building first advertised as Morgan's Hotel. Soon afterward, in 1874, the name was changed to City Hotel, and the hotel has been known by that name ever since.

The town had several major fires, and each played havoc with the red-brick hotel and other structures on both sides of Main Street. The townsfolk finally wised up and purchased a beautiful handpumper fire engine in San Francisco. The engine was called Papeete, and it still represents the community in various Firemen's Musters around the state.

Fire wasn't the only nuisance in George Morgan's career as an innkeeper. He almost closed the hotel once in a fit of anger after a thief stole a sack of flour from the kitchen. He didn't mind losing the fifty-dollar bag as much as he hated making the four-mile hike to Sonora and returning with another on his shoulder.

The City Hotel lasted until the 1930s, when mining activity faded, and was the last of Columbia's early hostelries to close. But it's now open for business again, this time under the management of the State Parks Department. The hotel has been completely restored and, where necessary, rebuilt and its historic brick façade has been retained. It is only one of Columbia's fine old frontier buildings now preserved as a State Historic Park.

The goal in restoring the City Hotel was to recreate as much as possible the old-fashioned atmosphere of an 1850-1870 Gold Rush hostelry. The parlor and nine rooms are furnished with unusually elegant antiques; some of the choice pieces come from the State Parks Department's own collection. One guest room has a large carved-fruitwood bed that came from the Bidwell Mansion in Chico, and the other rooms contain equally impressive pieces. Fresh-cut flowers, a daily newspaper and a breakfast of coffee and pastries are part of the fringe benefits to guests.

One reflection of the past is the short walk to the community showers. Each guest gets a robe and wicker basket that holds soap, towel, washcloth, and showercap. A hundred years ago, the miners took the same route, but they were given metal pans.

Some unique and exotically named drinks, inspired by the frontier setting, are served in the saloon. A beautiful brass cash register sits on the original cherrywood bar, which was shipped around the Horn from New England.

The dining room alone will bring the hotel much fame. The magnificent continental cuisine includes such special dishes as roast duck in orange sauce, lamb loin stuffed with spinach, and braised sweetbreads cooked with spring mushrooms. Depending on what you order, you may find much of it being prepared on a cart beside your table.

One interesting aspect of the hotel is that it serves as a training center for students taking hotel management courses at nearby Columbia Junior College. They work alongside the professional staff, and everyone is dressed in clothes of the colorful era that the hotel represents.

Columbia is not a static ghost town, although the entire community is a sort of museum for the way of life that existed during the mining era. Columbia is alive, and its businesses are operated as they were long ago. Visitors can participate in the old-fashioned activities by posing for a daguerreotype in hundred-year-old garb, panning for gold, attending a summer melodrama at Fallon House, or riding the Wells Fargo stage. Craftsmen still forge horseshoes at the blacksmith shop, and the daily newspaper is hand-printed at the *Columbia Gazette*. Tourists like the town because they can get involved and its history becomes all the more real.

City Hotel, Main Street, Columbia 95310. (209) 532-1479. Two-and-a-half miles north of Sonora on Highway 49; then 2 miles north on Parrotts Ferry Road. Lodging includes continental breakfast in the parlor; moderate. Nine rooms, each with half bath, community showers. Public dining room serves lunch Tuesday through Saturday 11:30 A.M.–2:00 P.M.; dinner Tuesday through Sunday 5:30 P.M.–9 P.M.; saloon open every day. Museum, shops, stagecoach rides in town. River running and fishing in the nearby Stanislaus River, Mercer Cave (15 miles), Moaning Cave (10 miles), Calaveras Big Trees State Park (29 miles); winter skiing at Bear West (Bear Valley). Columbia Firemen's Muster held in May.

SONORA INN

SONORA

In 1928 the Sonora Inn's fancy Victorian façade was hidden away behind a Mission-style front. The inn was only one of many California buildings that adopted the new Spanish appearance that was the current vogue. In the attempt to keep pace with the times, the inn has been improved more than most Gold-Country hotels, and it now incorporates all the conveniences expected by today's travelers. Sonora Inn is about the only hotel I know of in the Mother Lode country with an elevator. Nevertheless, the inn does have a historic past.

The ground that it sits on once bordered on the town plaza, a traditional feature of early Mexican villages. After the big fire of 1852 practically wiped out the flimsy town, the plaza was abandoned in favor of a uniform main street, eighty feet wide.

The first hostelry on the site was Mary Bailey's boarding house, established in 1854. A new law had been passed by the state legislature that allowed married women to carry on businesses in their own names as "sole traders." Mary was determined to test the law and became the first woman in the Mother Lode region to do so. Succeeding hotels on the site were called the American Hotel, the Sonora Hotel and the Stage Hotel.

In 1896 the palatial Hotel Victoria was built with rock hauled up from nearby Sonora Creek. It was an elegant, intricately decorated structure, elaborately furnished by its owner, Captain W. A. Nevills. He was quite proud of the hotel's modern conveniences, which included electric lights, fire hoses and a bathroom on each floor.

The Victoria was the end of the line for Wells Fargo stage passengers arriving by coach from the rail terminus at Milton. During one of these runs to Sonora in 1875, by the way, Black Bart robbed his first stage.

It would be nice if the Victoria's old façade still adorned the hotel, but what's done is done. In spite of the change in name and appearance, the Sonora Inn offers Gold-Country visitors everything they could wish for—good lodging, good food and good times. A lively bar and lounge features local musicians and a large dance floor. The Victoria Room is the classiest of the two dining areas where a wide variety of steaks and lobster are served. Weekenders to the area are addicted to the old hotel; they use it as a headquarters for their attendance at the popular annual events that have grown out of local history and tradition.

Sonora is a prosperous community and seems to be keeping pace with the twentieth century, but its frontier façades still add charm to the main street. Several interesting interiors have survived also, such as the beautiful apothecary fixtures in Mr. Brady's drug store. The hilly, crossroads town is a hub of activity all year long. In winter skiers traipse through on their way to the snow-covered slopes at Pinecrest and Yosemite.

Sonora Inn, 160 S. Washington Street, Sonora 95370. (209) 532-7468. One hundred and thirty-five miles east of San Francisco on Highway 108. Lodging on the European plan; moderate. All rooms have private baths. All meals are served to the public throughout the day, 7 A.M.–10 P.M. Swimming pool, bar and lounge, TV. Columbia State Park 4 miles, Sierra Railroad 4 miles. Fishing and rafting on the Stanislaus River; back roads lead to old mining towns; antique shops at Jamestown. Angels Camp Jumping Frog Jubilee and Sonora's Mother Lode Roundup held in May.

GUNN HOUSE

SONORA

The Mexican gold camp of Sonora was already a boomtown when Dr. Lewis C. Gunn arrived in 1849. The distinguished Philadelphian reached San Francisco by way of New Orleans and Texas and continued on to Sonora where the search for gold was in full swing. His background in printing and publishing led to an immediate partnership in the *Sonora Herald*, the first newspaper in the southern mining district. By the time his wife and four children arrived via Cape Horn two years later, he had a sturdy adobe home waiting for them. The structure, with two-foot thick walls, was the first two-story building of its kind in the town, which consisted mainly of wooden, hastily built shanties.

The family lived in the upper story of the adobe. The lower floor was filled with printing equipment and served as the newspaper's office. From here Dr. Gunn vigorously voiced his concern over political corruption and the abuse of civil rights, particularly those of the Chinese laborers who were being exploited in the greedy search for gold. His ideas were unpopular, as could be expected in such a rugged mining community, and the townspeople retaliated by burning his printing press.

Gunn's prior education in medicine made his services as a physician and surgeon invaluable to a steady clientele of banged-up and diseased miners. Gunn might have provoked disagreement as a newspaper man, but as a doctor he was widely respected. He served the community well until 1861, when he was appointed deputy surveyor of the Port of San Francisco and moved his family away from Sonora.

Dr. Gunn's adobe is now enveloped within the famed Gunn House Hotel complex, and it's difficult to believe the original is still there, expansion and remodeling has changed its character so. The two-story portion occupied by the hotel office is the original house and newspaper office. In the years after Dr. Gunn left town, the building was elongated and a balcony with columns was added across the front. In this form the structure served as Sonora's first hospital, the city hall, and later as the popular Italia Hotel.

By the 1960s the old building had been vacant and sadly neglected for some time. It was about to be wrecked when Mrs. Margaret Dienelt and her husband came to the rescue. Recognizing the adobe's underlying charm, they snatched it from the jaws of the wreckers and spent over a year restoring its beauty. Mrs. Dienelt poured all of her artistic taste into selecting the antique furnishings, many from

Mexico. These, along with the Mexican-style courtyard, paving tiles, and iron grill work, recall the Mexican heritage of the town's early days.

The rooms are all as interesting as the building itself, and are furnished with rich period pieces associated with the nineteenth century. The accommodations couldn't be more comfortable, and the modern luxuries such as TVs and ventilating grills are strategically placed to blend with the old-fashioned decor. Guests are so intrigued with the place that they often make advance reservations for the next year's visit before leaving.

Gunn House is actually a series of split-level structures, added through the years, that ramble up the hillside on three levels. The whole looks rather anachronistic in its setting amid the more contemporary structures along South Washington Street. But its historic appearance radiates an inviting charm that beats them all, without sacrificing any modern conveniences.

Gunn House doesn't have a restaurant, but there are several in the center of town only two blocks away. About ten miles east of Sonora, in the wooded little resort community of Twain Harte, is a very satisfying restaurant called Eproson House. I recommend it, along with the scenic drive through the pine-forested countryside.

Gunn House, 286 South Washington St., Sonora 95370. (209) 532-3421. Take Highway 108 to Sonora. Lodging only, inexpensive to moderate. Twenty-seven rooms, all with private baths. Swimming pool, TV, telephones. Columbia State Park 4 miles, Sierra Railroad 4 miles, fishing and rafting on the Stanislaus River, antique shops at Jamestown. Angels Camp Jumping Frog Jubilee, Columbia Firemen's Muster, and Sonora's Mother Lode Roundup, all held in May.

The Sierra

THE SIERRA

The roads leading into Yosemite National Park are constantly being improved and straightened, much to my chagrin. The old twisting routes were quite enjoyable and had more of the back roads feeling. But that's progress!

Once inside the park, you're faced with the single most dramatic stretch of nature in the entire Sierra range, and the number of visitors reflect its appeal. Yosemite is a wonderland of granite domes and peaks, valleys sculptured by ancient glaciers, meadows of wildflowers, giant sequoias, and waterfalls spilling over rocky ledges. Marmots scramble from rock to rock, and an occasional bear makes his presence known, particularly in the campgrounds where the garbage cans are usually rifled through nightly. Pesky mosquitos attack during late spring and early summer after the heat of the day thaws them out. As an introduction to the park, a copy of *Yosemite Road Guide* is invaluable. This booklet is keyed to roadside markers and explains the human and natural history of the park's features.

Spring is the ideal time to visit Yosemite Valley. The trees on the canyon floor are alive with fresh new leaves, and the melting snows cause the waterfalls to flow full force. In spite of the relaxing environment of the valley, the village shops and stores help create a beehive of activity that seems almost out of place there. A more restful retreat is at Wawona, in the southern end of the park. The old resort is not so overrun by people and is practically devoid of the busyness that plagues the Valley.

The Tioga Road is Yosemite's scenic link between the southern Gold Country and the east side of the Sierra. The route is open only half the year, though—it's snowbound from approximately late October until Memorial Day. Tioga Road makes a spectacular descent from the 10,000-foot Tioga Pass to the junction with Highway 395 near the shore of mysterious Mono Lake, sometimes called "The Dead Sea of America." The little town of Bridgeport is twenty miles north of the lake and a popular base for exploring the eastern Sierra slopes and the old ghost towns of Bodie, Masonic and Aurora. The grassy meadows around Bridgeport are filled with sheep during the spring, and Basque shepherds roving with their flocks make a picturesque sight.

An amazingly beautiful route northward along the eastern base of the Sierra leads to magnificent Lake Tahoe. The lake and its seventy-two miles of shoreline have long been one of the most popular recreation spots in the West. Its natural features are best enjoyed in the state parks that stretch along the western shore. Of primary interest to tourists are the sandy beaches, Fallen Leaf Lake, Vikingsholm Castle in Emerald Bay State Park, lake cruises, and the winter ski slopes.

BRIDGEPORT INN

BRIDGEPORT

Visting Bridgeport has become something of a biennial pastime for me. The setting in the grassy meadows surrounded by saw-tooth mountains is magnificent, and the town is a welcome oasis on the long stretch up Highway 395 to Tahoe. In spite of the encroachment of neon and asphalt, some of the town's early character still shows. The handsome courthouse was built entirely of wood in 1880 and is one of the rare examples in California of a finely detailed Italianate courthouse. Several Victorian residences and churches scattered around town also help to suggest some of the community's past.

My base for exploring the area is the Bridgeport Inn, built in 1873 by Hiram Leavitt and formerly called Leavitt House. Prior to building the hotel, Mr. Leavitt operated Leavitt Station, a few miles up the Sierra slope on the wagon route to Sonora Pass. As a skilled carpenter he knew his trade well, and the sturdy hotel is as sound now as when it was built. The exterior appearance has been altered only by an extension across the front added early in the century.

Some of the velvet-covered furniture in the downstairs parlor came around the Horn in the late 1880s. The beautiful pot-bellied stove once warmed hands and feet in the Miners' Union Hall at Bodie. For a long time the bottom portion sat in the parlor without its dome-like top. One day a local resident realized that he owned a stove top but no bottom, and the discovery was made that the two pieces belonged together. So the fancy stove is now complete and serves to warm the downstairs.

In the bar, the thick walnut slab, over which drinks are served, came from the ornate courthouse down the street, and was previously the County Clerk's desk.

I like moving about in an old hotel such as this —climbing the carpeted staircase, meeting people in the narrow corridors, jiggling the skeleton key in the door's primitive lock. Most of the rooms are modestly furnished. One, however, has a big carved bureau and an elegant matching bed which, they say, was slept in by Mark Twain during his rambles through the area as a newspaperman.

The intimate little dining room, with its simple wooden chairs and tables, has a more relaxed atmosphere than the newer places around town. The dinner house menu is basically steaks, lobster and prime rib.

After checking into the hotel, I usually drive the scenic eighteen miles to Bodie, the most authentic ghost town in existence. My visits to Bridgeport always include a trip to this venerable old relic of the past. On my third pilgrimage, a couple was getting married in the weathered wooden church. They were dressed for the era, and it was a scene right out of the old west. Many buildings of the deserted mining camp still stand, in various shades of disrepair. They are protected by the State Parks Department. Except for a resident ranger, the museum-like town has no inhabitants. It hasn't been restored, and it isn't a tourist trap—just a town that died and is frozen in a state of decay.

Aside from Bodie there is plenty in the back country to scout for, especially the numerous townsites and mines where you can retrace the steps of the miners. Strange tufa domes line the shores of Mono Lake, 24 miles to the south, and the Hoover Wilderness lies 15 miles to the southwest in the Toiyabe National Forest. Just north of town is Lake Bridgeport, a favorite with boaters and fishermen. The lake accounts for the unexpected seagulls that hover over this vacation-oriented community.

Bridgeport Inn, Bridgeport 93517. (714) 932-7380. From South Lake Tahoe drive 5 miles south on Hwy. 50, 47 miles south on Highway 89, and 41 miles south on Highway 395. Lodging on the European plan; inexpensive. Open all year. Six rooms with private baths, 10 rooms share two baths. Other motel units available. Dining room serves breakfast, lunch and dinner to the public during the summer months. Meal service varies during the winter. Forty miles to Yosemite.

AHWAHNEE HOTEL

YOSEMITE NATIONAL PARK

A few hundred years ago, the early inhabitants had a name for the incomparably beautiful canyon of Yosemite. They called it "Ahwahnee," which means deep, grassy valley. Many names that were prominent in the folklore of the Ahwahneechee Indians became associated with Yosemite's features, and the name Ahwahnee was given to the park's finest and most luxurious hotel.

Around 1925 the park directors decided that new accommodations should be built in the Valley to handle the influx of tourists that was expected to travel the nearly completed, all-year highway from Merced. Kenneyville, at the base of Royal Arches, was picked as the site. It had long been a transportation center, but its barns, corrals, and stables were rapidly becoming obsolete as automobile usage increased. Its location, however (adjacent to the meadows with the vertical granite cliffs as a backdrop), was perfect for the new country hotel. It was a proud day for architect Gilbert Stanley Underwood when the Ahwahnee was finished in 1927. The rugged, masculine appearance of the structure was the product of an era when buildings were designed to harmonize with their settings.

The new rapid motor route had been finished the previous year and tourists were attracted into the Valley as never before. The meadows were knee-deep with campers, and the overcrowding created situations that would make today's problems seem minor. To some extent, the Ahwahnee did alleviate the overcrowded conditions. However, the hotel's elegance made accommodations there only within the means of the upper classes.

Just walking down the rustic, slate-floored portico into the cavernous lobby is impressive. And the grand lounge certainly lives up to its Indian heritage. Geometric designs from the basketry of California tribes were used as basic design motifs, and they show up everywhere—in floor patterns, wall and ceiling ornaments, wrought-iron work, and stained-glass windows. Across the way is the enormous dining room with its tall picture windows and timber-trussed ceiling. This is the scene of the annual Bracebridge Dinner, a medieval Christmastime feast. People who know about this feast clamor to get on the waiting list far in advance.

For everyday dining, the luxury of the Ahwahnee is unmatched. This is one of the few country inns I've visited where you can have breakfast in bed or dinner in your room. But the real treat is dinner in the grand dining room under the warm glow of the chandeliers. The offerings include Chinook salmon poached in white wine, Long Island duckling marinated in brandy, rack of spring lamb roasted in herbs and garlic, prime rib served with Yorkshire pudding, and, for light eaters, an omelet with a choice of fillings.

Non-hikers will find all kinds of indoor and outdoor spaces for writing, sunning, playing games, or just sitting and gazing at the granite cliffs and fearless wildlife. The wings of the big rambling hotel reach out into the forest and are strategically located to give each room a spectacular view of the Valley's features. Off in the pines and across the rustic footbridge are several woodsy cottages sitting unobtrusively among the trees.

Visitors will notice that the Ahwahnee is cared for with great pride. Everything is impeccably maintained, just as it was in the old days when the hotel catered to those who knew the joys of fine living.

Ahwahnee Hotel, Yosemite National Park 95389. (209) 373-4171. Located at the east end of Yosemite Valley behind Yosemite Village. Lodging on the European plan; expensive. All 121 rooms have private baths; 24 cottage rooms. Open during all seasons. All meals served to the public. Dinner seatings at 6:30 and 8:30 P.M. (Reservations necessary). Dancing and nature films during the summer. Tennis courts, heated swimming pool, nine-hole pitch and putt. Spring Bike Rally in the Valley; 1189 square miles of spectacular national parkland; hiking, backpacking, climbing, fishing, winter skiing. Beautiful autumn foliage.

Years ago, an overly protective doorman admonished Herbert Hoover for entering the lobby in his dirty fishing clothes. The doormen are gone now, and the clientele is not as exclusive as it used to be, but the Ahwahnee still exudes all the luxurious grandeur it was intended to express. Some guests might feel the Ahwahnee is really a bit too grand at times, particularly when they find themselves dressing up for dinner. Such urban rituals may seem out of place in the mountains, but it's all part of the tradition and the elegant way of life reminiscent of an earlier era.

WAWONA HOTEL

YOSEMITE NATIONAL PARK

The rambling Wawona has seen a whole lot of history come and go. Even before Yosemite became a national park, the hotel was a major stopover on the rugged trek to the Valley. In the early days, travelers arrived at the hotel by stagecoach in a cloud of dust, tired and weary from a long day's ride. For forty years the Yosemite Stage & Turnpike Company served the hotel until the motorstages—the beautiful Pierce Arrows and Thomas Flyers—took over in 1916. But these new-fangled contraptions offered little more comfort, and the passengers eagerly looked forward to the restful serenity of the luxurious hotel.

The aggressive and hard-working Washburn brothers of Vermont were determined to make their fortunes in the West. They built a road from Mariposa over rugged Chowchilla Mountain and purchased the old lodging house at Clark's Station. The station was later renamed "Wawona," the Indian word for big trees. Unfortunately, a fire wiped out the Washburn's lodge in 1878, but a year later the Long White (Clark's Cottage) had taken its place. The complex grew; the

Main Hotel building and Washburn Cottage were added in 1885, and the Manager's Cottage in 1900. The long annex that stretches down toward the highway is newer, of 1917 vintage.

Wawona became a bustling center of activity as stages, freight wagons and passenger-laden coaches converged on the idyllic mountain resort. Among the distinguished guests were Presidents Grant, Hayes, and Teddy Roosevelt, as well as Horace Greeley and Williams Jennings Bryan. The dignitaries usually spent the night at the hotel before setting out to see the giant sequoias at the Mariposa Grove of Big Trees.

Today the hotel complex is a thing of beauty in the peaceful pines overlooking the meadows. The overall appearance hasn't changed much since the old days and the original character is still intact. The complex was purchased by the National Park Service in 1934, and the service has maintained the old-time atmosphere.

Among the most dominant architectural features are the wide verandas that encircle the buildings. All the rooms and suites open onto these breezy wooden porches. Inside the main building are sitting parlors, registration desk, and the dining room.

Breakfast is the meal I enjoy most at the Wawona, especially if I get up early when the sun is just beginning to filter through the tall trees. It's great to stretch on the open veranda and walk across the dewy lawns with the cool mountain air stinging the nostrils. Starting the day with bacon and eggs, steaming coffee, fresh jam on warm toast, and a view into the pine boughs through the many-paned windows of the dining room is a superb treat. Follow that with a long hike to Chilnualna Falls or through the Mariposa Grove.

For less ambitious hikers, the Yosemite Pioneer History Center is just down the hill. This is a collection of historic cabins and log buildings, moved to the site from various parts of the park and arranged as a typical village of Yosemite's past. The inhabitants dress in clothes of the era, carry on their primitive occupations, and are eager to answer questions about the old days.

The history of the pioneer village makes a fine complement to the history of the Wawona. This venerable hotel is the last of the grand mountain resorts in California, and one of the few still existing in the West.

Wawona Hotel, Yosemite National Park 95389. (209) 373-4171. Eighty-one miles north of Fresno on Highway 41, or 31 miles south of Yosemite Valley on Highway 41. Open April until Thanksgiving. Lodging on the European plan; inexpensive to moderate. Most accommodations with private baths or connecting baths; some rooms in the main building share community baths. Dining room open to the public for all meals. No pets. Nine-hole golf course, heated swimming pool, stables, Wawona History Center, Mariposa Grove of Big Trees, 1189 square miles of spectacular national parkland; hiking, backpacking, climbing, fishing.

MAYFIELD HOUSE

TAHOE CITY

Lake Tahoe has been famed as a resort area since the first hunting and fishing lodge was built there in 1862. In the first decades of this century, the arrival of the automobile and good roads led to increased de-velopment along the shores, particularly construction of fine new vacation homes for well-to-do Bay Area residents.

Norman Mayfield was one of the early con-tractors who set up business in 1925 and worked out of a large tent near the lakeshore. He was responsible for building many beautiful summer homes which in those days were designed to be totally compatible with their forest settings and were built entirely of indigenous materials. First rustic granite bases were constructed, then timber upper structures were covered with wood shingles or clapboard siding. The fancy interior beams and trusses were capped with wood shake roofs. Julia Morgan, architect for the Hearst Castle at San Simeon, worked closely with Mr. Mayfield; he constructed her grand designs for several wealthy clients.

In the mid-thirties, Mr. Mayfield built a residence for himself just a couple of blocks back from the shore in Tahoe City. It was not one of the grand designs; rather it seemed like a large cottage. Perhaps it was inspired by the Craftsman Movement of 1900-1920 which stressed simplicity, durability and harmony with natural surroundings as its principles. The stonework was laid up by the same stone mason that worked on the large estates nearby. Mr. Mayfield lived here through the years until recently when he offered the house for sale and moved to Southern California.

Joanne Neft, an admirer of many California inns, seized on the opportunity to fulfill a dream of having her own bed-and-breakfast place in an area short on such romantic retreats. The Mayfield House with its bungalow charm, sitting prettily under large pine trees was ideal.

Six guest rooms have been decorated in a style compatible with the age of the house. Each room has a name: the Mayfield Room and Julia's Room, on the upper floor, have king-sized beds and sitting areas. The cozy Guest Room is reached by its own small flight of steps and looks out over the front yard. The Study is one of three rooms on the ground floor. The walls have wood paneling, the windows are covered with plaid drapes and fresh flowers sit in copper pots in the library alcove.

The large living room has a beamed ceiling and is furnished with a comfortable leather-covered sofa and chairs making it a pleasant place to relax and read the morning paper or plan the day's events. The huge stone fireplace takes the chill out of skiers returning from the slopes.

Behind the house is a tree-covered terrace, perfect for breakfast on warm sunny days. Guests are well fed with magnificent delights such as sweet-potato muffins, French cheeses, homemade pastries, fresh fruit, orange juice, and steaming coffee.

What changes the Nefts made to the interior of the house were so tastefully done that even Mr. Mayfield has approved. He made a return visit for the open house held by the Nefts so that members of the community could get a glimpse inside the beautiful home that had stirred their curiosities for so long. Not only did Mr. Mayfield express his approval of the new changes, he also celebrated his ninety-first birthday as a part of the festivities.

Mayfield House, 236 Grove Street, Tahoe City 95730. Mailing address: P.O. Box 5999. (916) 583-1001. Approximately one-half mile north of junction of State 89 and State 28. Lodging includes breakfast for guests only; moderate. Three downstairs rooms share one bath, three upstairs rooms share one bath. Beaches, waterskiing, golf courses, hiking, Sugar Pine Point State Park (10 miles), D. L. Bliss S.P. (15 miles), Emerald Bay S.P. and Vikingsholm Castle (18 miles), M.S. Dixie moonlight dinner cruise (South Shore-30 miles), winter skiing. Numerous restaurants around Tahoe City.

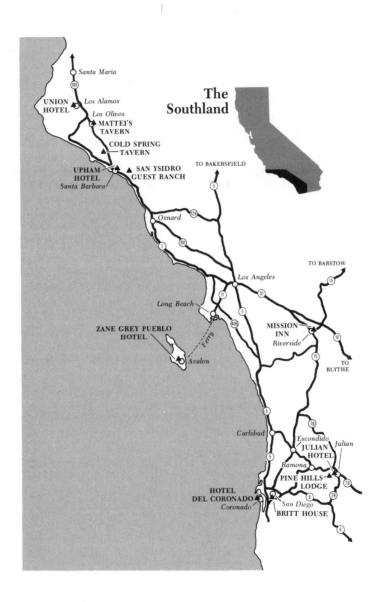

The
Southland

Santa Maria

UNION
HOTEL
Los Alamos
Los Olivos
MATTEI'S
TAVERN
COLD SPRING
TAVERN
UPHAM
HOTEL
SAN YSIDRO
GUEST RANCH
Santa Barbara

TO BAKERSFIELD

Oxnard

Los Angeles

TO BARSTOW

Long Beach

ZANE GREY PUEBLO
HOTEL

Ferry

Avalon

MISSION
INN
Riverside

TO
BLYTHE

Carlsbad

Escondido
JULIAN
HOTEL
Julian

Ramona
PINE HILLS
LODGE

HOTEL
DEL CORONADO
Coronado

San Diego
BRITT HOUSE

THE SOUTHLAND

On my trips into the Southland, I found that several areas remain relatively unchanged and reflect the gentle scenic beauty of their nineteenth-century settings. The Santa Ynez Valley is one such area. The rolling grassy hills are dotted with cattle and beautiful Arabian thoroughbreds grazing on the oak-studded farms and ranches. Several country towns have managed to hang onto their few remaining antique buildings. Worth seeing are the false-fronted stores at Santa Ynez, the little red schoolhouse at Ballard, Mattei's Tavern in Los Olivos, the old general store at Los Alamos, and Mission Santa Ines on the edge of Solvang. Solvang, although touristy, is quaint because of its overall Danish architecture and heritage.

Further east, Santa Barbara is a colorful Mission town with more charm than most cities of equal size. Its adobe-style buildings with their red tile roofs add a definite character. Numerous shops and restaurants are found tucked away in Spanish courtyards and in old buildings, some dating back to the early 1800s.

Another nice region of unspoiled terrain and interesting back roads lies between Riverside and San Diego. Since the coastal route is mostly cluttered with beach homes, I suggest an inland tour through the following places: to Perris (trolley museum), Temecula (antique shops), Pala and Pauma Valley (Indian missions); up the forested slopes to the Mt. Palomar telescope (gallery and exhibit hall), through the foothill towns of Santa Ysabel (superb bakery) and Julian (mine tour); and south through the forest and meadows of Cuyamacho Rancho State Park to Descanso, along Lyons Valley Road to Jamul, and on to San Diego.

The climate all along the southern coast is rather kind to tourists. Summer days are warm, but evenings are cooled by the ocean breezes. Winter is short, and snow sometimes falls on the distant mountain ranges.

UNION HOTEL

LOS ALAMOS

The little town of Los Alamos was by-passed several years ago when the freeway slashed through the countryside of Santa Barbara County. Since then, most tourists have traversed the area unaware that they were missing a quaint little California town with a row of antique shops and one of the few old-fashioned general stores in the state. And now there is a special reason for making the short trip off the beaten path: The Union Hotel is back in business. The proprietor, Dick Langdon, set out to recreate a piece of old America, and considering the progress he has made so far, he will have much success.

The original Union was a wood-frame building built in 1880. It became a popular stopping place, since it was located on a heavily traveled stagecoach route between Santa Barbara and San Francisco. The builder was J. D. Snyder, a New Yorker with an impressive business expertise that enabled him to carry on a variety of ventures while simultaneously acting as local agent for Wells Fargo & Company. Using his farming profits, Snyder built the hotel, giving every detail of its operation his closest attention.

The original hotel had a short life, however: it burned to the ground in 1886. In 1915 it was rebuilt on the same site; Indian adobe was used and the walls were made eighteen inches thick. The establishment struggled through the twentieth century in various guises—as the Hotel Los Alamos, a pool hall and dance hall, and a rooming house for oilfield workers. It was also boarded up for nineteen years.

Twenty-five owners later, Dick Langdon purchased the hotel and vigorously began to restore it. An old sketch of the original Union guided Langdon in reconstructing the façade to match the original. Well-aged wood from twelve old barns was used to create a worthy replica of the front. This remarkable piece of handcraftsmanship was the work of Jim Radhe, a cabinetmaker by trade and now a permanent resident of the hotel. Langdon discovered Radhe's talents soon after the hotel was purchased; he liked watching the way Radhe worked and offered the woodworker a permanent job if he ever needed one. Two weeks later, Radhe showed up at the front door with his suitcase and has been around ever since, continuously executing his employer's ideas for interior and exterior restoration.

Inside, the lobby is as much a museum of early Americana as it is a hotel foyer, filled with some really amazing pieces—for example, the hundred-year-old gaslights from a Mississippi plantation, a hand-chiseled mantel from an old mansion in Pasadena, and a handmade lamp used in the movie *Gone with the Wind*. At the rear of the lobby is the dining room, a real drawing card. Most visitors become well acquainted with the fresh, homemade, family-style meals put together by the owner's wife, Teri. Dinner guests are welcome to browse through the upstairs parlor and twelve rooms when they aren't being used. All the guest rooms contain rather interesting nineteenth-century four-poster beds.

Constant changes are taking place at the hotel as Langdon adds one amenity after another. Following breakfast, guests are taken for a ride around the Los Alamos area in a 1918 White-made touring car. This fifteen-passenger vehicle, of the vintage that replaced stagecoaches in the early part of the century, was originally built to serve Yellowstone National Park.

The vacant lot adjacent to the hotel has given way to a pleasant outdoor garden with a sixty-foot grape arbor, brick paths, and beds of colorful flowers. The highlight is the quaint Victorian gazebo. At night the floor is raised hydraulically to reveal a Jacuzzi large enough for twenty guests.

The latest addition to the scene is Raz, the pet crow. Langdon's familiar whistle is all it takes for Raz to come flying to his master.

The Union Hotel is Langdon's hobby, and he has attracted much attention with his accomplishments. The dining room recently accommodated a group of one hundred drivers testing a fleet of new cars in the area. Weddings are a popular occurrence in the enchanting gazebo. Hollywood personalities have been guests at the hotel, and the interiors were even used as the setting for a forthcoming movie.

I like Dick Langdon's philosphy: "My goal is to make this the nicest old hotel in America. I have the rest of my life to do it, and I'm in no hurry, because I'm going nowhere. So, if Jim and I can't do it right, we don't do it."

Union Hotel, 362 Bell Street, Los Alamos 93440. (805) 344-2744. Forty-five miles northwest of Santa Barbara via Highway 154 and U.S. 101. Lodging includes breakfast; moderate to expensive. Two rooms have private baths, ten rooms share community baths. Pool table, outdoor barbeque, swimming pool. No pets, no children except in dining room. Dining room serves dinner to the public Friday and Saturday, 5 P.M.–9 P.M.; Sunday, noon– 8 P.M. Hotel and dining room are closed Monday through Thursday except for private parties. Antique shops in town, Danish town of Solvang 19 miles, La Purisima Mission 15 miles, scenic back roads. Los Alamos Olden Days and Solvang Danish Days festivals both held in September.

MATTEI'S TAVERN

LOS OLIVOS

When he wasn't ranching or roping wild deer, Felix Mattei was giving deep thought to the future of beautiful Santa Ynez Valley. The Swiss immigrant soured on the dairy business and turned his attention to the inevitable encroachment of the Pacific Coast Railway into the fertile grain-growing region. He hoped to capitalize on the impending influx of businessmen and travelers, being the first to provide accommodations at whatever location the railroad chose as its terminus in the area. After some snooping around, Mattei determined that the newly established town of Los Olivos would be the most likely site, and here he built his modest, two-story Central Hotel in 1886. His vision paid off. The railroad's terminal was built directly across the street a year and a half later.

With business from the railroad and two stagelines, the hotel was a big success. In 1888 a big new luxury hotel was erected down the street and threatened to draw away customers. But by then Mattei's fine gourmet restaurant had such a widespread reputation that people went to the new hotel only when there was no room at Mattei's. The fancy hotel burned to the ground a couple of years later and Mattei's competition was gone. That year he changed

the name to the Hotel Los Olivos and enlarged the building to look much as it does today.

Plenty of colorful events took place at Mattei's. One night in 1891, for example, a lynch mob stormed into the hotel. They had been informed that a couple of prisoners, men who had killed the local station agent, were being held there by the sheriff. The hotel was cleared of guests, and the sheriff and the two murderers slipped out among them disguised as women, and were long gone before the crowd got wise.

As often happens in the course of progress, the railroad eventually left the small town behind. It continued south to Santa Barbara, and the side trip to Los Olivos was abandoned. The stagelines folded and the hotel seemed headed for the same destiny. But the age of horseless carriages arrived just in time, and with the new-fangled machines came the publication of tour guides. They raved about the hotel's fine accommodations and dining room, and Mattei's fears were diminished.

Famous people were among the arrivals. The old registers show the signatures of a Vanderbuilt, a Rockefeller, and a Lorillard. Herbert Hoover and William Jennings Bryan were guests, as were many movie stars, such as Clark Gable, Bing Crosby, Marjorie Main, and Rosalind Russell.

Felix Mattei died in 1930 and a three-mile-long funeral cortege paid tribute to his popularity as an innkeeper and a friend. As an appropriate memorial, his family changed the name of the hotel to "Mattei's Tavern."

Although Los Olivos is only a remnant of the town it used to be, the tavern has survived and is the main attraction. Many visitors to the Danish community of Solvang drive the five miles to have dinner at the tavern's famed restaurant. The rooms no longer accommodate travelers and there have been other changes over the years, but not the kind of changes that mar the historic atmosphere. Waiting for a table will give you a chance to look around the rustic old lounge at photos and maps from early days, and at the portraits and paintings done by Felix's son Clarence.

For dinner, you'll find yourself either in one of the dimly lit interior rooms, which are very plush and sophisticated, or on the sunporch, which provides a greenhouse setting, with lots of windows, and white wicker tables and chairs. Menu selections include such superbly prepared entrees as Hawaiian Chicken, scallops, Teriyaki Steak, mahi-mahi, or a slab of prime rib that will knock your eyes out. A lettuce and tomato salad is tossed at tableside, and there is a good selection of wines to choose from. The restaurant is now operated by Chart House Enterprises, a company noted for its fine establishments in historic old buildings across the country.

Old-timers may not consider the food comparable with the authentic home-style cooking of Mattei's era, when dinner was made with fresh vegetables from the backyard, fruit from the orchard, and newly caught trout from the nearby creek. But a visit to the tavern is still a marvelous dining experience at a true nineteenth-century stagecoach inn.

Mattei's Tavern, Los Olivos 93441. (805) 688-4820. Thirty-five miles northwest of Santa Barbara on Highway 154, or 5 miles north of Solvang. Restaurant only. Dinner served Monday through Friday, 6 P.M.; Saturday and Sunday, 5 P.M. (reservations advised). Saloon open Monday through Friday, 5 P.M.; Saturday and Sunday, 12 P.M.

COLD SPRING TAVERN

SANTA BARBARA

The most rustic inn I've found in California sits beside a horseshoe bend in the old Stagecoach Road just a mile off busy Highway 154. A twenty-minute drive north from Santa Barbara will take you back about a century in time to a shady canyon and the old weathered buildings of Cold Spring Tavern.

In its youth, as the Cold Spring Relay Station, the tavern was a welcome refreshment stop on the long stagecoach trek between Los Olivos and Santa Barbara. The Concord wagons, pulled by four-horse teams, hauled passengers, Wells Fargo Express boxes, and the U.S. mail to its noontime stop at the station. After lunch and a stretching of legs, two more horses were added to the team for the big pull over San Marcos Pass and on into Santa Barbara.

This routine went on between 1868 and 1901, and these were years of excitement. Bandits would strike at the station while the teams were being changed, grab the Wells Fargo box at gunpoint, then beat it up the canyon with the posse in hot pursuit. And historic figures rode the line. For example, Susan B. Anthony, the noted suffragette, arrived at the station one day riding atop the driver's seat in her billowing skirts because the coach was full.

Today the tavern is still surrounded by several old buildings of the same log-and-shingle construction. What is now the Log Cabin Bar was a bottling plant at one time, where the sparkling mountain water from Cold Spring was bottled and sold as "the purest water in the county." The little gift shop was a "bedding-down room" for the weary stage drivers who had time to catch a few winks. The transplanted Ojai jail hides behind a big fence. It was built of laminated planks in 1873 and was trucked across three mountain passes to its new site under the big bay trees.

The tavern operates as a restaurant and bar these days, serving lunch and dinner throughout the afternoon and evening. Lunch is mostly a choice of sandwiches or chili, and the chili is a favorite with regular customers. The dinner menu is inspired by the setting; examples of entrees are Cold Spring Chicken or Tavern Red Snapper. The Stagedrivers Choice is a juicy concoction of pork sautéed with sherry, mushrooms, apples, bacon, and spices. All items come with soup or salad, potato or rice, vegetables, and homemade tavern bread.

The red-checkered table cloths provide about the only color against the monochromatic, weathered plank floors and walls. The rickety interiors of the dining rooms are decorated with a collection of stuffed animals, branding irons, clocks, historic photos, and some unusual antique pieces that have a history of their own.

Outside, under the big trees, are logs and tables for eating and drinking, or sitting and relaxing. People drive up from Santa Barbara just to loll away an afternoon in the old-fashioned atmosphere of the shady glen.

Cold Spring Tavern, 5995 Stagecoach Road, Santa Barbara 93105. (805) 967-0066. About 10 miles northwest from Santa Barbara on Highway 154 to the arched bridge just beyond San Marcos Pass, then right on Stagecoach Road for 1 mile. Restaurant only. Open daily. Lunch, 11 A.M.– 4 P.M. Dinner, Sunday through Thursday 5 P.M.–9 P.M.; Friday and Saturday, 5 P.M.–9:30 P.M. (Reservations suggested.)

SAN YSIDRO GUEST RANCH

MONTECITO

Up in the foothills above Montecito, on what was once a great rancho owned by the Franciscan Missions, is one of the oldest guest resorts in California. It officially opened as a hotel in 1893 after friends of Harleigh Johnston, then the owner, talked him into providing cottages so they could spend the summers and mild winters basking in the sun and riding along mountain trails. Johnston settled here in the 1880s and found the climate and soil just right for growing fruit trees. Now the old stone citrus-packing building is the dining room, and below it the old ranch winery has been made into the Plow and Angel Bar.

Left over from land-grant days is the little original adobe house, built in 1829 and one of the oldest buildings in the Santa Barbara area. It was dedicated as an historical landmark in 1964 by the Native Sons of the Golden West. The adobe belonged to padres from the Santa Barbara Mission who farmed this fertile region until it passed into private ownership. Now, a couple of the old guest registers, one from 1893, are kept in the window of the house.

Quaint wood-frame and stone guest cottages with such names as Geranium, Oak, Outlook, Upper and Lower Hillside, are all surrounded by grassy lawns and gardens, bright patches of flower beds, and clipped shrubbery.

The fame of the ranch is obvious from the impressive list of guests who have enjoyed its privacy. Sinclair Lewis, Aldous Huxley, Ogden Nash, and Somerset Maugham were some of the noted writers. John Galsworthy revised his *Forsyte Saga* during a visit. Among others were Maxfield Parrish, the Cabots, the Lodges, Bing Crosby, Jack Benny, Groucho Marx, Sandy Koufax, Eric Sevaried, Hubert Humphrey—the list is endless. The late President and Jacqueline Kennedy chose the ranch for their honeymoon. Vivien Leigh and Lawrence Olivier chose it as the site for their wedding.

Guests and their families can keep an active schedule with ranch barbeques, picnics, games, or trips to the beach and the busy streets of Santa Barbara, about six miles away. Or they can choose to maintain strict privacy. The secluded, woodsy setting has a magnificent backdrop; the Santa Ynez Mountains step back in fading layers. The surrounding canyons are ribboned with bridal paths and hiking trails, and the country lanes leading into town are great for after-dinner walks.

Nostalgic recollections from my own days on a ranch were stirred by the sight of the horses, their handlers, and the stables. These outbuildings, down by the creek, house the American quarter horses available for guests. Trails fan out into the 525 acres of woodland terrain, and sometimes trailside barbeques are prepared for the riders. San Ysidro Ranch is one of the few places in California I've visited that has horses available for guests, and the beautiful animals give the resort a true ranch feeling.

San Ysidro Guest Ranch, 900 San Ysidro Lane, Montecito 93108. (805) 969-5046. Four miles east from Santa Barbara on Highway 1 to the San Ysidro Road exit, then north to Mountain Road, then right to the ranch. Lodging on the European plan; expensive. Dining room serves all meals to the public. Thirty-nine guest cottages, Plow and Angel Bar, dancing, swimming pool, children's wading pool, playground, riding, tennis on the grounds. Golf, beaches nearby.

UPHAM HOTEL

SANTA BARBARA

After checking into my room on the second floor of the Upham Hotel, my curiosity moved me to climb the steep stairs to the enclosed "widow's walk" rising above the roof. There must have been a great view of the wharf in the old days, but trees and buildings now obscure the vista. On a clear day, you can barely see the sun reflecting on the Pacific.

The Upham, with its old-fashioned hospitality, has been around for a long time. Only in Santa Barbara could such a small country hotel survive for so long in what is now the heart of the city. It's the oldest guest house in a city once famous for its great resort hotels—places such as the Potter, Arlington, and San Marcos. The Upham outlived them all, undaunted by even the most ferocious of Santa Barbara's earthquakes. Thanks to the flexible redwood frame, only a couple of the old hotel's chimneys toppled during the big shake of 1925. The greatest inconvenience suffered there was the lack of cooking gas. For three weeks meals were prepared outdoors by the Chinese cooks and served to guests under the trees.

The hotel was built in 1871 by Amasa Lyman Lincoln, and was known as Lincoln House. Mr. Lincoln was a transplanted Boston banker who soon grew tired of the lonely life on a rancho west of Santa Barbara and moved his family into town. His concern over a lack of accommodations prodded him to build a New England-style boarding house. For the architect, he chose Peter J. Barber, a noted designer of many classic Victorian homes in the city. Barber created a handsome building in the Italianate style with hand-fashioned brackets under wide eaves. The columned veranda on two sides of the building had ornate scroll-like capitals. A schooner brought redwood from the mills at Santa Cruz, and the lumber was floated ashore, since Stearns Wharf wasn't built until a year later.

The site was basically countryside in 1871, and the city has gradually grown up around the two-story clapboard inn. Amazingly, its appearance has changed little since it was built. An annex was constructed about the turn of the century and several cottages were added to the grounds around 1911, creating some pleasant outdoor patios and cloistered garden spaces.

On my visit, after a night of peaceful relaxation, I took an early morning stroll around the shady residential neighborhood of nineteenth-century homes before returing to the hotel for breakfast. The dining room, located in the annex, is at the end of a garden path that winds along under a vine-covered arbor. Local residents as well as hotel guests can vouch for the Upham's long-standing reputation for good food.

Back in the main house and adjacent to the lobby desk is a portion of the veranda which has been enclosed to form a sunroom. Here light beams through many panes of glass. Across the way is the large antique-filled living room that looks out into the garden. The guest rooms are snug, and although some are not furnished with period pieces, others have nice old antiques.

The hotel has had several owners, and Cyrus Upham was the last to pin his name on it, replacing the classier Lincoln House. Regardless of the name, it's a remarkable achievement that this small historic hotel is still active in a day when so many quick-service motels beckon to the passing traveler.

Upham Hotel, 1404 De La Vina, Santa Barbara 93102. (805) 962-0058. Two blocks west of State Street at Sola and De La Vina. Lodging on the European plan; moderate to expensive. Fifty rooms, most have private baths. Breakfast, lunch and dinner served to the public. Close to Santa Barbara Mission, ocean beaches, El Paseo shops, historic adobes. Old Spanish Days held in Santa Barbara in August. Sunday art shows along the beach.

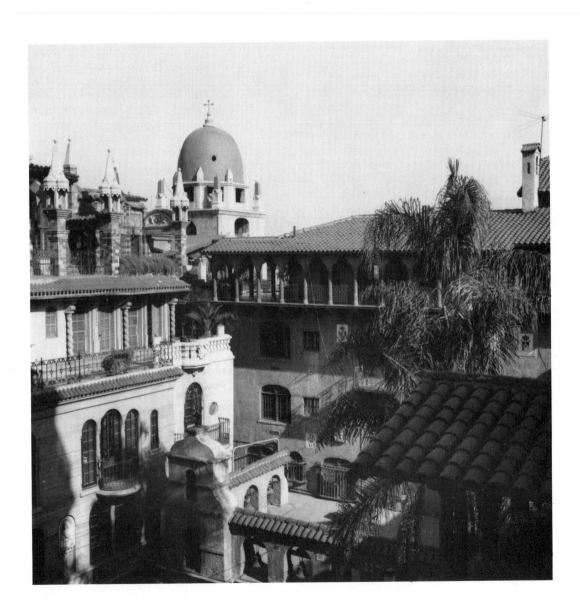

MISSION INN

RIVERSIDE

Friends had told me that they never fail to visit the Mission Inn whenever they set foot in Riverside, and I discovered why. I find it difficult to describe the experience of staying at the Mission, for it would take a book to tell the complete story behind one of the most fascinating inns in America. It may not exactly fit the category of a country inn, but it did grow out of one. And the memories of a visit will remain long after smaller inns have been forgotten. Mission Inn is more than an inn. It's a monument to the Mission Revival style of architecture, a museum for the amazing collections of its creator, Frank Miller, and one of the truly bizarre buildings of the world.

To understand the inn, you have to understand Frank Miller. He was a highly energetic person who was virtually born into the hotel business—his father owned the small Glenwood Hotel in Riverside. Miller was a poetic and a self-made man, and through his studies he developed a great love for California and its history. He was particularly fascinated with the history of the missions and the compassionate padres who devoted their lives to helping the poor savage Indians. He admired the mission structures for their significance as places where the needs of every passing stranger were filled. He therefore had a fondness for the mission's architectural style.

As a civic-minded citizen intent on leaving his mark on the community, Miller set out to upgrade his father's Glenwood Hotel, which had become a very popular part of the Riverside tourist scene. In 1901, together with architect Arthur Benton, Miller watched the Mission Inn evolve according to his plan.

All the features and design motifs, the arches, flying buttresses, campaniles, and vaulted rooms were borrowed from the California missions and incorporated in the inn's architecture. Miller had a way of dramatizing his accomplishments and a knack for having things turn out right. Consequently, the inn became famous. It was also the first major example of Mission Revival architecture—a style that would soon afterward sweep the country.

Frank Miller vowed to introduce the people of California to the various cultures of the world, and he traveled extensively around the globe in search of furnishings for the hotel. He sent back exotic artifacts, antiques, rare art treasures, and more than a few items that seemed to be nothing more than junk to the folks back home. But Miller knew what he was doing. His eye caught the unusual and indigenous architectural features of foreign lands, and as wing after wing was added to the hotel, it became more international in appearance.

For those who visit the inn today, one of the daily guided tours is a must. It's the only way to see the fascinating architectural maze, much of which is inaccessible to the public otherwise. The guide leads visitors through the St. Francis Chapel with its ornamental screen covered in gold leaf, the unusual Lealea Room guarded by a nineteenth-century Buddha, the long Music Room with its 2000-pipe organ, the Garden of the Bells, Writers Row, and the various rooms housing priceless collections.

I found the inn to be one of the most rewarding stopovers in all my travels. I felt the atmosphere of a grand hotel from the minute I entered the cavernous lobby. After I checked in at the long wooden desk, the elevator took me to the fourth floor, and I followed the winding walkway along the brink of the elaborate interior courtyards to the rooftop pentprogram. The inn's original appearance—from the days when kings, queens, presidents, and Hollywood's most prominent stars enjoyed its hospitality—is currently being restored.

The inn covers a full city block and has its own attractions to keep guests occupied. At street level are several galleries and specialty shops, such as the Parrot and Freckled Frog. The Mission Inn Dinner Theater, in the basement, combines dining with a theater performance. The inn also has another fine dining room, which opens onto the Inner Court, where guests can enjoy meals or drinks outside under brightly colored umbrellas.

Riverside itself is the largest of southern California's inland cities. Numerous city parks, golf courses, green rolling hills, along with thousands of trees that line the streets, make the community a major oasis on the edge of the desert. The surrounding countryside is a forest of orange groves. The "parent" Navel Orange Tree, from which all other navel orange trees in California have descended, still thrives in its own little park in the center of the city. There are many historic buildings to see, many cultural programs to enjoy, and numerous attractions in nearby Los Angeles and Orange County, only an hour away.

house suites. My comfortable room was unlike any I had stayed in before. The Moorish fireplace, giant arched window, plank-and-beam ceiling of formed concrete, and the beautiful paintings on the walls combined to give a feeling of lavishness not expected for the modest rate. The experience is well worth a trip off the beaten path.

Like many historic buildings, the Mission Inn saw a period of slow decline. A date with the wrecker's ball was an almost certainty until a sympathetic group, dedicated to preserving old, but usable buildings, stepped in and began a vigorous revitalization

Mission Inn, Seventh and Orange Streets, Riverside 92501. (714) 784-0300. Forty-four miles east of Los Angeles via Interstate 10 and U.S. 60. Lodging on the European plan; moderate to expensive. 25 rooms have private baths, 2 bridal suites. Dining Room serves lunch and dinner and Sunday brunch. Dinner Theater. Guided tours daily at 11:30 A.M. and 2:30 P.M., also at 3:30 P.M. on Sunday. Swimming pool, ground floor shops in hotel. Museum across the street; several historical buildings nearby.

ZANE GREY PUEBLO HOTEL

AVALON

Zane Grey considered Catalina to be something of a paradise. His insatiable love for deep-sea fishing brought him here many times in search of marlin, fighting tuna, and particularly great Pacific sword-fish. He held numerous records from time to time, and the best catches were immortalized in his collection of fishes, now at the New York Museum of Natural History.

A brief honeymoon on the island was the first introduction to Avalon for Grey and his wife Dolly.

As the town and island became more and more popular as a resort area and a haven for deep-sea fishermen, Grey returned time after time. His sentiments for the place grew, and he eventually purchased from the Wrigley family an impressive site high on a hill overlooking Avalon. In 1926 he built a Hopi-pueblo-style home on the promontory, highly authentic in appearance and detail, and radically dissimilar from the beautiful Victorians belonging to other islanders. The house was Grey's own statement, and a reflection of his fascination with the Indian cultures and their building styles. It came to be a home away from home and was used primarily as a summer house when Zane Grey and his brother, R. C., fished the waters around Catalina. A cottage was later added for R. C. across the patio from where the swimming pool is now located.

Zane Grey's days on the island were a source of inspiration to him, and he did a good deal of writing here. Dolly was away in Europe the year the house was built, so he channelled his efforts into producing page after page of thrilling accounts of the old West. In this home, as in his other nomadic retreats in Arizona, Oregon, and Southern California, stood a Morris chair in which Grey sat and wrote. He turned out all of his manuscripts in longhand on a wide board placed across the arms.

After Grey's death the house had a succession of owners, and the old adobe lost some of its primitive character. But it still has enough charm to intrigue guests. It became the most interesting lodging in Avalon when the present owners converted it to a small inn around 1960. Most of the guest rooms are located on each side of the long corridor. Some have spectacular views of the harbor and town, while others overlook the chaparral-covered hills. At the end of the hallway is the living and dining room with its big adobe fireplace and log mantel. The plank door and dining table were hand-hewn, and the rustic teak ceiling beams were picked up on a Tahitian fishing trip and brought back to the island aboard the *Fisherman*, a boat that Zane Grey bought in Nova Scotia in 1924.

On my visit to the Pueblo, I stood on the covered deck outside the living room and gazed in awe at the magnificent harbor village below me. It's rumored that the Wrigley family had second thoughts after selling the property to Zane Grey, and tried to buy it back. I could see why.

Guests at the small hotel will find as much tranquility and solitude in the sea and mountain

environment as Zane Grey did during his visits to the island. What's more, they will have the thrill of knowing that everyone's favorite western novelist slept here.

Zane Grey Pueblo Hotel, P. O. Box 216, Avalon 90704. (213) 510-0966. Catalina Island is accessible from Long Beach by boat (Long Beach/Catalina Cruises [213] 832-4521) or by air (Catalina Airlines [213] 548-1314). Lodging only; inexpensive to moderate. Seventeen rooms with private baths. Transportation provided to and from the dock or airport. Swimming pool, complimentary coffee and toast, living room with TV and piano. Pets specifically prohibited. Island and coastal tours. Beaches, shops, movies, restaurants, stables, tennis, skin diving, fishing nearby.

JULIAN HOTEL

JULIAN

I like the quaint little town of Julian, tucked away in the foothills of San Diego County. Julian is only a small town and doesn't have a need for the franchise trade or flashy neon signs and plastic fronts. The old-fashioned appearance of the community makes it the occasional backdrop for episodes in television series. Numerous old buildings provide much of its charm —wooden grain towers, steepled churches, very old stores, a stone museum, and the neatly painted Witch Creek School, which was moved into town and now serves as the local library.

The town's real gem is the Julian Hotel, a

simple Victorian beauty that dates back to 1887. The original portion of the building was built by the Albert Robinson family, freed Georgian slaves who came west with their friends, the Baileys. Drew Bailey laid out the town, but named it after his cousin Mike Julian, because Mike was "purtier."

The Robinsons were a thrifty couple and channeled all their savings into a small restaurant and bakery which eventually became the Hotel Robinson, later renamed the Jacobs Hotel and finally the Julian Hotel. The surrounding area was the scene of a rousing Gold Rush during the 1870s. The Eagle Mine, on the outskirts of town, is one of the few remaining traces of this activity. Today the owners offer guided tours through the maze of tunnels.

At one time, the bustling mining community had a population larger than San Diego and as many as seven hotels. But fire had a way of leveling wooden buildings, and only the Julian Hotel has survived.

In its glory days, Julian was a stopover on the transcontinental stage route between Yuma and San Diego, and many stagecoaches rumbled through the town depositing passengers at the hotel's doorstep. Some of the guests were famous; the names of U. S. Grant and Admiral Nimitz show up in the old registers.

The town pretty much rolls up its sidewalks after the sun goes down, but guests can linger in the rocking chairs on the front porch and chat, or engage in a game of checkers in the downstairs parlor. The hotel rooms are charmingly decorated with Victorian-style wallpaper and huge four-poster beds and bureaus. At the end of the hall are the ladies' and gentlemen's "Necessary Rooms." Behind the hotel, a one-bedroom cottage has been charmingly restored with a Franklin fireplace, wicker furniture and lace curtains.

On the frosty morning of my recent stay, I awoke to the smell of fresh-perked coffee permeating the hallway. A handsome old stove spilled out its welcome warmth. After an early breakfast at the nearby cafe, I enjoyed a walk along sunny Main Street as shopkeepers busily swept the sidewalks in front of their folksy, false-fronted stores. Everyone here seems to take pride in preserving this portrait of rural America, a scene that is getting harder and harder to find.

Visitors will find a diversity of landscapes around the town. Highway 78, leading east, descends into a spectacular canyon and then out onto the desolate lowlands of the Anza-Borrego Desert. The terrain south of Julian is a mixture of oak and pine forests and grassy meadows in the Cuyamacho Rancho State Park. Apple orchards, to the west, have replaced the mining activity, and roadside fruit stands sell delicious honey-colored cider. Weeds seem to be getting as much attention as the apples these days. During the Julian Weed Festival, held in August, residents create ingenious arrangements from the seemingly useless plants, and they are placed on display in the town hall.

Julian Hotel, Julian 92063. (714) 765-0201. From San Diego take Interstate 8 east to Highway 79; then drive north 23 miles. Lodging only, inexpensive to expensive. One cottage, fifteen rooms, two with private baths. Restaurant at Pine Hills Lodge. Close to museum, mine tour, fruit stands, Cuyamacho Rancho State Park, Anza-Borrego State Park. Wildflower Show in May, Apple Days in October.

PINE HILLS LODGE

JULIAN

The sign on the highway says "worth looking for." It's a fairly challenging game of hide-and-seek, though, as you drive the couple of miles down the meandering country road toward the secluded community of Pine Hills. The lodge is nestled on a knoll surrounded by large oaks, pines, and sycamores, and the area comes alive with color when autumn rolls around. The old main building, several cottages, and recreation hall are all woodsy, shingle-style structures—the epitome of the word "rustic."

The original cabins, which no longer exist, were unique, to my knowledge. Each was built as a shingled treehouse: a wooden stairway led to the cottage perched approximately fifteen feet above the ground. Some stairs were circular with cantilevered treads wrapping around the tree trunks. Others led upwards from platform to platform with benches built into the pole construction. At the top of a giant pine tree sat an unusual observation tower, the only one of its kind in California, reached by a circular stairway. At the lodge's elevation of about five thousand feet, the views from these various vantage points must have resulted in a spectacular panorama of the surrounding countryside. But the treehouses are all gone now; they have been replaced with the present cabins, which bear names such as Blue Jay, Pine Cone and North Star.

Down the hill from the lodge is the recreation hall, outfitted as a gym in earlier days. It served as a temporary training camp for Jack Dempsey when he was preparing for his first big bout with Gene Tunney, held in Phildelphia on September 23, 1926. Dempsey, incidentally, lost the fight along with his championship title that night.

The big wooden lodge is a survivor of the original complex built around 1913. The huge stone fireplace is the center of attraction; it's a friendly gathering place for conversation or for impromptu bluegrass and country music sessions. Or guests can just sit and listen to the old player piano and watch the fire. The adjacent dining room has a woodsy interior that looks out on the treetops, and is about the only locale for distinctive dining in the area. On the walls of the bar next door, are some nostalgic photos taken at the lodge soon after it was built. I can't vouch for the upstairs guest rooms, but I understand they are quite rustic also, with shared baths.

Pine Hills was one of the favorite hideaway resorts during the twenties and thirties, when city

No other lodge in California had tree houses like the ones that perched in the trees around Pine Hills Lodge in the 1920s and '30s.

folks trekked over the rough mountain roads from Los Angeles and San Diego for their share of the backcountry experience. The roads are a lot better now, but the hideaway possibilities are as good as ever.

Pine Hills Lodge, Julian 92036. (714) 765-1100. One mile west from Julian on Highway 78, then 2 miles south on Pine Hills Road. Lodging on the European plan; inexpensive to moderate. Lodge rooms share baths; several cottages. Dining room serves dinner to the public Wednesday through Sunday. Sunday brunch. Close to museum, mine tour, fruit stands, Cuyamacho Rancho State Park, Anza-Borrego State Park. Julian Apple Days festival in October. Popular bakery at nearby Santa Ysabel.

HOTEL DEL CORONADO

CORONADO

There was a time when more than a dozen Victorian resort hotels existed in the coastal countryside between San Diego and San Francisco. Fire and hard times were the chief contributors to their demise, and only one of these luxurious rambling inns still serves the public. The Hotel del Coronado survived both types of disasters, since the owners were financially able to keep its doors open during the war years, and to install a magnificent fire-sprinkling system in 1916.

The story of this hotel is unique. It begins in San Diego's land-boom days when Elisha Babcock and H. L. Story decided that the potential of the long windswept spit of land across San Diego Bay was greater than its then current use as a hunting ground for jackrabbits. They purchased the Coronado Peninsula in 1885 at a fantastically low price. Their plan was to divide the land into town lots and construct an elegant resort hotel as the center of attraction. Mr. Babcock immediately sent for Indiana architects James and Merritt Reid to come west and design a structure that would be the talk of the western world. They agreed, and in March 1887, even before formal blueprints were completed, construction was started and carried on in an around-the-clock operation.

The mostly unskilled workers, recruited from San Francisco's Chinatown, plugged away steadily in almost a trial-and-error fashion, but their craftsmanship gradually improved as construction progressed. Eleven months and one million dollars later, the hotel was complete enough to open for business. The first guests signed in on February 18, 1888. Toil and sweat had produced the largest wooden building in America and a classic example of the Queen Anne style of architecture. It was the first hotel in the world to have electric elevators and an electrical lighting system. Thomas Edison himself was on hand to personally supervise the installation.

Nowadays, the Saturday afternoon tours will give the first-timer an intimate view of what the hotel is like and how it operates. Our guide was a friendly and amusing chap who enticed us through the dazzling spaces with his interesting, anecdotal stories about the illustrious guests and incidents from the past. He also pointed out some details, often glossed over, in the Del's finely wrought interior: the vaulted wooden ceiling of the Crown Room, gilded elevator cage, wood-panelled lobby, and elaborately carved gazebo that had been shipped around the Horn.

The romantic old hotel can't help but intrigue you with its red shingle towers and lacey trim, fronted by an endless stretch of sandy ocean beach. Across the avenue is the little boathouse, also built in 1888 and just as highly decorated as the hotel. The boathouse was recently completely renovated and moved closer to the shore, and it is now a nautically inspired restaurant overlooking the colorful yacht harbor.

As elegant as it all may seem, you don't have to be a president, king, Prince of Wales, or even a struggling movie star to stay in this historic landmark. The room rates are suited to everyone's budget, but you may have to settle for one of the streetside rooms instead of an oceanfront suite with a private veranda.

At the turn of the century, a tent city flourished on the sand dunes while the hotel's interior was being remodeled. The natural outdoor setting next to the rolling surf was so popular that the temporary community thrived well into the 1930s. The beach still extends unmarred for miles in both directions, and watersports of all kinds continue to be a main attraction. The hotel's management can advise guests in arranging for sailboat rentals and deepsea fishing charters.

Is the Del Coronado a country inn? Well, it was in the old days before Mr. Babcock's land sales sparked the inevitable encroachment of civilization. Its grand scale may seem overwhelming compared to the smaller inns described in this book, but it does offer an experience that is unforgettable for its fantasyland resort qualities.

Hotel del Coronado, Coronado 92118. (714) 435-6611. Located on the Coronado Peninsula across the bay from San Diego. Take Highway 75 from Interstate 5 and cross the toll bridge to Orange Avenue. Lodging on the European plan; moderate to expensive. All 399 rooms have private baths. Two restaurants serve all meals to the public. Victorian Charthouse 1887 Restaurant one block away. Tennis, swimming pool, beach, TV, telephones, cocktail lounge, memorabilia room at the hotel. Guided tours of the hotel are given on Saturday at 1 P.M. Old town San Diego, Mission, Harbor Excursion, San Diego Zoo, Sea World, several museums, and ocean beaches nearby. Whalewatching at Cabrillo National Monument in December and January; Cabrillo Festival in September.

BRITT HOUSE

SAN DIEGO

Among San Diego's romantic attractions are the city's colorful Victorian homes. The most eye-catching of all is the huge Villa Montezuma, recently opened to the public as a museum. Several Victorians threat- ened by demolition were moved to Heritage Park, adjacent to Old Town, where careful restoration has preserved their beauty. Throughout San Diego's older neighborhoods, other Victorians are on display, not only as private residences, but as antique shops, professional offices and boutiques.

Of particular interest to visitors in the city is the resplendent Britt House, San Diego's only bed and breakfast inn. Beyond the multi-gabled exterior, this proud Queen Anne tower house has an extravagance of stained glass windows and elaborate interior woodwork. It was built of redwood around 1887 for Eugene Britt, an attorney. The mansion was recently purchased by Daun Martin and her husband Robert Hostick, together with their friends, the Michettis. Their visits to several fine California inns inspired them to create an equally charming hotel in their own town. Several months' worth of sanding, refinishing and wallpapering went into sprucing up the guest rooms. The owners were still painting and planting right up until five minutes before the house opened to the public for the first time.

All guest rooms retain the natural character of the Victorian's early days. Each room was given a name reflecting its prior use or the special feeling of the room. Four rooms including the Music Room, Library Room and Garden Room are on the first floor. The Governor's Room is furnished with pieces from the home of former governor Robert Waterman. Guests climb the magnificently detailed wooden stairway to the second floor where five more rooms are located. King Ludvig's Room is the most theatrical in appearance while Island View provides a glimpse of Coronado Island across the cityscape.

Breakfast, served either in the downstairs dining room, in the garden or on a tray in your own room, is truly a delight to look forward to. Fresh-from-the-oven breads are usually served along with jams, fresh-squeezed juice and a Viennese blend coffee. Some mornings, instead of the breads, guests will get wholewheat-hazelnut waffles topped with whipped cream, or porridge with raisins.

Fortunately, Britt House is only a two-block walk from San Diego's most visited attraction, Balboa Park. Many of its buildings were built for the 1915 Panama California Exposition. Today they house the Aerospace and Natural History museums, Hall of Science, art galleries and the Globe Theater. The world-famous San Diego Zoo is also located in the park.

Britt House, 406 Maple Street, San Diego 92103. (714) 234-2926. Lodging includes breakfast for guests only; moderate to expensive. Nine rooms share four baths. Theater and restaurants within walking distance. Roller-skating, tours of vintage vessels at the Maritime Museum, Harbor Excursion, Mission San Diego de Acala, Point Loma lighthouse.